LORETTE WILMOT LIBRARY
Nazareth College of Rochester

Rochester City Ballet

BOOKS BY ELLEN SWITZER

How Democracy Failed
There Ought to Be a Law
Our Urban Planet
Dancers! Horizons in American Dance

Dancers!

Dancers!

HORIZONS IN AMERICAN DANCE

BY *Ellen Switzer*

Photographs by
COSTAS

ATHENEUM *New York* 1982

LIBRARY OF CONGRESS CATALOGING IN PUBLICATION DATA

Switzer, Ellen Eichenwald.
  Dancers! : horizons in American dance.

  Bibliography: p. 269.
  Includes index.
  1. Dancing. 2. Ballet. 3. Dancing—United States.
4. Ballet—United States. 5. Dancers. I. Title.
GV1594.S94   793.3   82-1701
ISBN 0-689-30943-0   AACR2

Published simultaneously in Canada by
McClelland & Stewart, Ltd.
Composition by Dix Type, Inc., Syracuse, New York
Printed and bound by Fairfield Graphics, Fairfield, Pennsylvania
Calligraphy on the Title Page and Part Titles by Anita Karl
Designed by Mary M. Ahern
First Edition

To Jesse Morgan Switzer

Contents

3 · A Dancer's Education and Life

4 · Today's Young Dancers

5 · The Superdancers

Dancers!

Introduction

It is the movement of people and things that console us. If the leaves on the trees did not move, how sad the trees would be. . . .

—EDGAR HILAIRE GERMAIN DEGAS,
a great French painter who
loved to picture the human body in movement,
and who specialized in drawing and painting ballet
dancers.

WATCHING DANCERS indeed consoles me when I am sad. It also inspires me to get back to work when I feel lazy or burned out, lifts my spirits when I feel depressed, and adds a whole exciting dimension to my life. Knowing that I will see a ballet in the evening can make my whole day. Many of the ballets about which I write I have seen over and over again. But there is something new for me in every performance. Many of the dancers surprise me again and again, no matter how frequently I have watched them in performance, at rehearsals or in class.

I am what people call a balletomane, literally someone who is crazy about dancing, especially ballet. Balletomanes will spend the last ten dollars in their wallets on a ballet ticket and will, as a result, go without lunch for a week. We will travel miles on a bike, if necessary, to see a performance. And most of us will pass up any date (except to go to the ballet) in order to see a good dance company on television, even for the fourth rerun.

What is it that fascinates us about dance and dancers? The

beauty of this particular art form, of course. Many of us also love music, and dance is music with another dimension: the carefully planned but seemingly natural and inevitable movement of human bodies to the sounds we hear.

Many dances tell stories. Such classical ballets as *Swan Lake* and *Giselle* present fairy tales with princes, princesses, magicians, good and bad fairies and other characters that, in themselves, might fascinate nobody but a six-year-old child. But the integration of music, movement and the kind of emotional overtones that a really good dancer can invest in those unbelievable characters on stage transform what might be considered a rather simple-minded play into great art. After all, many of Shakespeare's plays (including Romeo and Juliet, which has been translated into innumerable ballets by choreographers of many countries) also have plots that on the surface make about as much sense as the average soap opera. In the case of Shakespeare, the beauty of the language, the poetry, elevates an unbelievable plot into a great play. In the case of dance, a combination of many different art forms—music, acting, dancing, scenery, costumes and lighting—create the special magic.

In recent times, the plotless dance has received the attention of the best choreographers. Often these dances tell a story too, but it's up to the individual viewer to determine what that story is. As dancer-choreographer Peter Martins once said about one of his ballets: "You see what you think you see." At their very best, these plotless dances become three-dimensional music, with tantalizing hints of profound meaning. The choreographer and the dancer make up part of the performance: you have to think about what that particular dance means to *you.* Frequently the same dance can take on different meanings when it's performed by a different dancer or a different company. In this way, even though one sees the same choreography many times, it can be a new experience every time.

Many of us also feel that there is something special about dance and dancers. It is impossible to be a dishonest artist and also a good dancer. In a world where so much is second-rate, where actors who can't act become stars, singers who hit false notes become celebrities, and writers of truly bad books become millionaires, it is impossible to survive as a bad dancer. Dancers not only have to face the exacting criticism of their teachers, their colleagues, and the ballet master for every movement they make, they also have to face themselves, literally, in mirrors that surround every dance studio.

And no matter how much a performance has been praised by the audience, the critics and his or her fellow dancers, I have yet to meet a dancer who is completely satisfied with what he or she has done. It's in the nature of dance to look for perfection, even though the dancer knows better than anyone else that perfection is not attainable . . . it's always somewhere out of reach. The perfect turn or jump exists somewhere in the back of the dancer's mind. He or she has never done it or even seen it done. But it's there all right, and the dancer will spend a lifetime trying to achieve it.

Watching someone who has spent a decade training his or her body into a fine-tuned machine and his or her mind to make that body do the seemingly impossible while looking as light and natural as a snowflake is what keeps balletomanes going back to the theater, usually more often than either time or budget permit.

And our number is growing. Within the past decade dancing has developed into one of the most important forms of artistic expression in this country. According to choreographer and dance historian, Agnes de Mille, there are now more than four million dance students in the United States. Of course, many of these young people take up dance in the same way they would take up swimming, skiing or baseball, as a form of sport or recreation. There are probably still many young girls who are going to ballet classes at their mothers' insistence because mom thinks ballet will improve their posture. (Actually that's probably not true. Most dancers walk with feet turned out. For posture, swimming is better.) But, every year, from two to three hundred thousand youngsters take the kind of advanced dancing classes that they hope will lead to a career in a ballet company, a modern dance group, on Broadway, or in films.

Dance has found an ever-increasing audience. In 1981, more people went to dance performances than went to baseball games. There are still many excellent dance groups that perform in high school and college gymnasiums or in church basements, on floors that are either too hard or too uneven for their feet, without proper lights, costumes or scenery.

Performances by nationally and internationally known companies take place in large theaters and are frequently sold out, as anyone who has ever tried to get a last-minute ticket to a performance by the New York City Ballet, the American Ballet Theater, the Dance Theater of Harlem, the Twyla Tharp Dance Company or the San Francisco Ballet will testify. Some ballet companies have managed to achieve that somewhat dubious state of popularity that includes having a regular group of scalpers lurking around the entrance before every performance. Scalpers are the ticket speculators who buy, either through subscription or by standing in line early in the season at the box office, large numbers of tickets, which they then resell just before the performance at illegally inflated prices. Formerly they confined their efforts to sports events and Broadway hit shows that were always sellouts. These days enterprising scalpers seem to buy up blocks of tickets to the American Ballet Theater performances featuring such superstars as Mikhail Baryshnikov and regular Friday and Saturday night performances of the New York City Ballet. Since they show up season after season, it may be presumed that they find their activities profitable enough to continue.

Ballet has always had an audience in Europe. In the Soviet Union tickets to dance performances, even by relatively unknown provincial companies, are very hard to obtain. Tourists report that a ticket to the Bolshoi in Moscow or the Kirov in Leningrad is a true prize. The Royal Danish Ballet is always sold out, as is the Royal British company. But sold-out dance performances in America are a relatively new development.

There are obvious reasons for this new popularity. Dance in general and ballet in particular have developed into a thoroughly American art form. Many of the best dancers and choreographers today are Americans, and dance, more than any other art form, truly reflects the American melting-pot qualities. The new choreographers, even those who were born and trained in other countries, like George Balanchine and Peter Martins, have become fascinated with all kinds of American music from jazz to classical, from Broadway show tunes to the Western square dance. Many are translating classical ballet steps and movements into uniquely American dance patterns. And American dancers seem to be stronger, faster and more agile than those trained in any other country including Russia, which has been thought traditionally to produce the best-trained dancers in the world.

The dance audience is also becoming younger and consider-

6

ably less exclusive. The gala performance, with its two-hundred-dollar tickets, still draws the society folk dressed up in evening clothes. But the tickets that sell out first are those in standing room, and young people wait in line for those seats, sometimes all night long. One sees more young people in blue jeans at any given performance of the New York City Ballet or the Alvin Ailey Dance Theater than one does matrons in mink coats and diamonds.

And, if dance has become more popular in the United States, it has also become better. Popularity has not ruined or even cheapened this art form, as it has so many others. Dancers in the chorus of some of our best companies can now accomplish feats of daring and skill that would have been impossible for the international stars of only ten years ago. What's more, today's dancers are taught to listen to the music: the high jumps and fast turns that somehow cause many Russian dancers to come down on the wrong note to the wild applause of their audiences, are not encouraged by American ballet masters. Here the music, whether it's a Gershwin show tune or a Mozart rondo, is an integral part of dancing. It is no wonder that the dance companies of other nations, including such outstanding organizations as Germany's Stuttgart Ballet, often feature American dancers or dancers trained in American dance schools.

So life is getting better and better for all of us balletomanes. One would think that we would not wish to advertise our enthusiasm since tickets for the best performances are already hard to get. But it's part of a balletomane's nature to want to recruit as many new members as possible to their ranks. That is one of the purposes of this book. Knowing more about dance and dancers will, I hope, bring young people who have not given this art form much thought into the theaters. After all, the state of the world being what it is, we can all use some consoling at various times in our lives.

1 Dancing: Its History

CHAPTER I

Where It All Started

Dance: to glide, step or move through a series of movements, usually to music . . . .
—THE NEW MERRIAM-WEBSTER POCKET DICTIONARY

PEOPLE have probably danced ever since they walked. In fact, many scientists believe that dancing may have preceded man on the evolutionary scale: certain animals, like insects and birds, go through recognizable patterns of movement as part of their courtship rituals.

At any rate, the earliest cave paintings show dancers, as do vases found in Egyptian and Greek tombs. Of course, we don't know what these dances looked like. One of the special qualities of dance is that, basically, it's movement. A picture can show a certain frozen moment in time: a stretched leg, a lifted arm, a jump . . . but, until the invention of the motion picture camera in this century, it was impossible to know what came before or after the pictured frozen second.

Dance seems to have served many functions for our long-ago ancestors. It was obviously part of religious ceremonies. There were dances that apparently mourned the dead and others that celebrated weddings. There were dances that seemed to celebrate a good harvest and others that seemed to implore some rain god to save the crops from failure and the people from famine.

In ancient Greece, dance was used to help train soldiers. It seems that football coaches who are insisting that some of their players take ballet or modern dance lessons are not so original after all. More than two thousand years ago some generals apparently knew that dance movements could strengthen muscles and promote the kind of flexibility and agility needed for hand-to-hand combat (the only kind used by early Greek armies).

We know that dance *performances,* with one set of people dancing while another set watched, were part of early Greek theater. We also know from pictures and descriptions that some of these dances imitated real life situations: wars, hunts and harvests, for instance. Other dances told stories, including some early myths. Gods, elves and gnomes, feats of heroism and magic seem to have played an important part in those early dances, just as they did in the nineteenth century ballets, like *Swan Lake,* that are still part of most large ballet companies' repertories.

In the Middle Ages, tumblers and acrobats were among the strolling players who traveled from town to town, gathering an audience wherever they could. Again, we have drawings and vivid written descriptions of these performers who, as part of their act, danced.

The fourteenth century probably saw the first attempts to turn dance from a social event or a religious ritual into an art form. According to many dance historians, France was the country in which those who were charged with providing suitable entertainment for the court first began to look at the English and Bohemian dances regularly performed in the towns and village squares, to polish the steps and patterns they saw, and to formalize them into choreographies that could be copied and repeated. French is still the language of the dance world. All the steps and movements that are used in today's ballets have French names and some dance historians feel that this happened because France was truly the cradle of dance as an art form.

By the beginning of the fifteenth century, dance masters from France and Italy were traveling throughout Europe teaching basic steps to groups of dancers at various courts. Good dancers were in great demand at the many castles and courts where princes and dukes vied with each other to provide special entertainment for their guests. At the time when a young boy or girl had little chance of escaping from the grinding work and poverty of peasant life, learning to be an excellent dancer was a way to improve one's lot in society. When the dance master came to the village to look for possible recruits for his company, the fourteenth and fifteenth century stage mothers were only too pleased to bring their children to these informal auditions to show off what grace, strength and agility their youngsters might have.

The word ballet was apparently used for the first time in 1489, when the Duke of Milan gave a huge feast to celebrate his marriage to Isabella of Aragon. As each course of the wedding supper was brought in, dancers appeared as mythological characters associated with the dish being served. For instance, while the guests were eating their roast lamb, the dancers gave their version of the story of Jason and the Golden Fleece. When fish was served, Neptune appeared surrounded by a group of sea sprites. To top off the evening, the guests saw a special ballet celebrating the joys of love and matrimony.

At the French Court, dancing became the most popular entertainment during the seventeenth century, in the time of Louis XIV. Louis was apparently an early balletomane. In his youth, he participated enthusiastically in the dances. He starred in twenty-seven different ballets, including one in which he appeared as the sun . . . and that is where his nickname "the Sun King," originated. He organized entertainments that often lasted all night, and once even appeared as a dancer in a ballet before the general public.

After becoming tired of dancing himself, he also seems to have tired of watching his corps of amateur aristocrats dance, and decided to found the first school of dance: the Académie Royale de Danse, organized to teach court ladies and gentlemen to dance better, and later expanded to admit a few talented commoners to its classes. A few years later, the school was expanded again to include musicians and actors along with dancers, and renamed Académie Royale de la Musique. By now almost all the students were commoners, who would perform professionally at court entertainments.

Other European monarchs also danced publicly in ballets. The Duke of Monmouth, the illegitimate son of Charles II, danced a ballet at court during the time he was commander-in-chief of a British army battalion. Even William of Orange, that staid and sober Calvinist, danced in his youth in ballets put on by the Dutch court in Holland.

During these court performances dancers wore masks, probably because, in spite of its popularity, dancing as part of a performance was still considered slightly immoral, especially when the company was a mixture of the top nobility and the despised professionals. One may assume, however, that the audience knew who was dancing what.

About seventy-five years later, a dancer-choreographer, Jean Georges Noverre, took dance from the realm of casual court entertainment to what he considered a serious art form. He insisted that all dancers must be highly trained professionals; that choreographies should be serious dance dramas instead of a form of pageant or variety show; that masks made no sense, and that costumes should be especially designed to permit the dancer to move freely, rather than conform to the fashion of the day. Choreographies should be based on character and situation, there should be a clear relationship between the music and the movement of the dancers; and a dance drama or ballet should be created as a permanent work of art, to be danced by many companies, rather than as a one-time entertainment for a special occasion, he insisted. The professional dancer, especially the highly trained female dancer, was the star of Noverre's entertainments.

By the middle of the eighteenth century, ballet companies were securely installed in most of the important European capitals. In Russia, Empress Catherine, with ambitions to create a major culture capital in St. Petersburg, built a special theater for the dancers she attracted from all over Europe. Frederick the Great, the king of Prussia (an unpleasant man and a mediocre monarch in spite of the flattering adjective tacked onto his name, but a great patron of the arts), also encouraged ballet performances at his new opera house in Berlin. Paris still remained the dance capital of the world, but other countries began to organize their own ballet groups, to hire choreographers, to commission music and to develop their own scenery and costume designers.

Even more significantly, some performances were public. They took place in theaters, not in private court ballrooms, and among the newly emerging European middle class, dance found patrons who were willing and able to pay to see a performance.

By the late eighteenth century, choreographers, dancers and audiences had decided that stories featuring enchanted princesses, hapless country maidens, charming or not-so-charming princes, ghosts, elves, magicians and other extraordinary creatures made "pretty ballets." By the middle of the nineteenth century, the story ballet, usually a tragedy of doomed love, was the main attraction of dance stages throughout Europe, and ballet was beginning to be seen on other continents including the United States.

This was the time of romance, of passionate love, of moonlit scenery, and of sad fairy tales that were supposed to have the same effect on the audience as today's three-handkerchief movie. Often the stories of these ballets were too absurd to be taken seriously even by the most dedicated romantic, but by now the art of choreography and the techniques of dancing were highly developed, and if the audience did not really believe these stories in which maidens died of unrequited love and princes walked off cliffs to their deaths with swans who were actually enchanted princesses, they admired what they saw on stage sufficiently to keep coming back for more.

Several ballets from this period can still be seen in today's ballet programs: *La Sylphide,* the story of a ghostly girl who seduces a mortal hero away from his equally mortal fiancée; *Swan Lake,* the story of a prince who falls in love with a princess turned into a swan by an evil magician; and *Giselle,* the story of a treacherous prince who seduces a sweet but sickly peasant girl and pays for his treachery by being almost danced to death by a band of roving *wilis,* spirits of maidens betrayed by their lovers.

Several themes run through these ballets. Love usually ends in tragedy. Simple peasants are noble; aristocrats are often corrupt, everything takes place in idealized, slightly misty settings. Very similar themes ran through the novels, poems, operas and paintings of the times. And, since ballet depends to a great extent on music to achieve its effects, composers were writing the kinds of pieces that were right for the dancing these stories required.

Another important factor had been added to ballet: the point shoe. At first women dancers had danced in heeled shoes, just like male dancers. Then during the eighteenth century, they began to move around in flat dancing slippers. Finally in 1770, a dancer called Anne Heinel was described as appearing on a "stilt-like toe tip." Other dancers tried to imitate her technique. At first they were held on their toes by what the ballet producers hoped were invisible wires. Later, dancers discovered that they could dance on point (on their toes) by acquiring larger slippers than were required for their feet and stuffing the front of these

slippers with cotton wool. By the middle of the nineteenth century, ballet dancers were wearing foot gear that looked like the
ballet slippers worn by today's ballerinas. And well before that
time certain basic steps and positions had been formalized as the
basis of all choreographies.

Dancing on the tips of her toes made it possible for the ballerina to perform all kinds of athletic and artistic feats that she
had not been able to accomplish when her heels were still firmly
planted on the ground. She could turn faster, hold unlikely bal-
ances, jump noiselessly and seem often to be suspended in midair. Because the stories the ballets told usually centered around
tragic women, the male dancer was often an antihero. Not only
did he not dance on point, he also betrayed innocent maidens,
chose the wrong girl for his bride and generally behaved in a
manner not worthy of the heroine who loved him. In *Giselle* the
prince disguises himself as a commoner in order to win the love
of the heroine, only to walk out on her with his royal fiancée. Of
course, when she dies (presumably of a broken heart), he is very
sorry. He is sorrier still when the *wilis*, the ghosts of maidens
who have died as a result of betrayal and unrequited love, try to
force him to dance himself to death. (This, incidentally, makes
for one of the few really spectacular male solos in nineteenth
century ballet). He leaves the stage, heartbroken but redeemed,
when the ghost of Giselle, who has forgiven him his treachery,
implores the chief *wili* to allow her lover to live.

In *Swan Lake,* the prince, who falls in love with the princess
turned into a white swan by an evil magician, allows himself to
be fooled by the same magician into asking a witch turned into a
black swan to marry him, thus causing the death of the white
swan princess. The audience will, of course, forgive him his mistake at once. The white swan princess and the black swan witch
are always danced by the same ballerina, so it does not seem
extraordinary for the prince to believe that his true love has just
gone home to change her dress. But never mind, the black swan
is a different girl, and because the prince has broken faith with
the white swan princess, she must die. In this case he dies with
her . . . they walk off the cliff into the Swan Lake together.

Some of the best-known of the woman dancers became international stars. In spite of the fact that travel was difficult,
several of the more intrepid ballerinas seem to have moved from
one royal court to another. Carlotta Grisi, an Italian, became a

sensation with the Paris Opera Ballet. Another Italian, Marie Taglioni, made it all the way to Australia via Paris; and a Viennese-born dancer, Fanny Elssler, brought ballet from her native country to America, via London and Paris.

By the midde of the nineteenth century, the romantic ballet was firmly established in most European capitals. The choreographies, costumes and scenery varied, of course, but there were some general principles that were usually followed: a passionate romance ending tragically; a misty, mysterious setting; and an imposing central character, the ballerina. Men choreographed, ran companies and managed outstanding female dancers.

CHAPTER II

The Russians

Aurora notices an old woman who beats on her knit-
ting needles a 2/4 measure. Gradually she changes to
a melodious waltz in 3/4 time, but suddenly, a rest.
Aurora pricks her finger. Screams, pain. Blood
streams . . . give eight bars 4/4, wide. She begins to
dance—dizziness—as if bitten by a tarantula, she
keeps turning and then falls unexpectedly, out of
breath. This must last from twenty-four to thirty-two
bars. . . .

—From the exact instructions given by MARIUS PETIPA,
choreographer of the Russian Imperial Ballet,
to Peter Tschaikovsky on how to compose a section
for the ballet, *Sleeping Beauty.*

T HERE WAS a time not very long ago when ballet, to
most people, meant Russian ballet. Actually ballet came to Russia relatively late, and it came bringing traditions and styles from
many other countries, most especially from France and Italy. But
once ballet came to the Imperial Court at Leningrad, it found an
enthusiastic and generous patron in the Tsar himself. In fact in
the middle of the nineteenth century, Tsar Nicholas I of all the

Russians was prepared to spend a great deal of money on the dance companies that had been developing in his country, both in the capital at St. Petersburg (now Leningrad) and in Moscow.

There had been some dancing at the court of Catherine the Great, but the real beginning of Russian ballet, as we think of it today, came in the year 1847, when a young French dancer, Marius Petipa, received from the Imperial Theater an offer of the job of principal male performer at the then unheard-of salary of ten thousand francs per year.

When he arrived in St. Petersburg, Petipa found a well-trained and eager company. The dancers were actually employees of the Imperial household, just as were the footmen and other servants. Many had been selected from families of serfs. Some were still serfs. But most had learned ballet techniques from early childhood. They had the talent and training of some of the best Western European dancers without their difficult temperaments. Since they were regarded as servants of the Tsar, they were not spoiled by attention and glamour. They worked hard, did what they were told and were able to accomplish technical feats that had rarely been seen on the stages of Paris, London or Vienna. What's more, Petipa found that the male dancer had an important role in the Russian company.

The Tsar knew exactly what kind of ballet he wanted. He asked for choreographies that combined romantic stories with a luxury and pomp that had not been seen on stage since the royal spectacles of the Sun King. To get the kind of entertainment thought suitable, he was willing to pay as much as was necessary for elaborate scenery, luxurious costumes, choreography and music.

Within a few short years, Petipa moved from the position of principal dancer to chief choreographer. Under his leadership, Russia became the dance center of the world, a position it would hold for the next sixty years at least.

Over a period of thirty years, Petipa created more than forty full-length ballets, some of which still survive. He also arranged dances for thirty-five operas and revived and recast seventeen ballet productions choreographed earlier by other European masters. It is Petipa's version of *Giselle*, for instance, that we still see today.

Petipa taught dozens of young men and women to perform choreographies of almost incredible complexity and difficulty for that time. Because he had so many good dancers, he specialized in a new form of story ballet. There was a main couple, often a prince and a princess, and a story line. But there was always also a gigantic festival or entertainment inserted in the ballet as part of the story. As part of the entertainment (which was known as a divertissement), other talented young dancers, usually members of the corps, were given a chance to perform solos, duets or dance in groups of three or four. In this way, Petipa was able to bring along a promising dancer, using him or her for small solos, then major parts in a divertissement, and finally, in a starring role. This meant that when one of the top performers was injured or became too old to dance the difficult choreographies Petipa devised, there was always a new, young, fresh one to step into his or her shoes.

As Petipa worked with his ever-improving group of dancers, he refined and further formulated many of the steps, turns, movements and jumps that are still the raw material of ballet. He also came to the realization that a ballet was probably about as good as the music to which it was danced. Until he took over the Tsar's companies, there had always been an official company composer. Often this was a man who got his job through influence and favoritism. The best composers hardly ever applied for the post. After all, they wanted their music to be the star of any performance, not a dancer. Many had refused to compose for dance because they considered dancing to be entertainment, while, naturally enough, they thought of their music as art.

The official composer at the time of Petipa was a Hungarian, Ludwig Minkus. He managed to produce some highly serviceable scores, though his music does not stand up to much listening on its own. But one of the greatest of the nineteenth-century composers was working in Russia during the time Petipa was revolutionizing the ballet. Tschaikovsky was writing symphonies and concertos, piano pieces and songs that were moving, beautiful and dramatic beyond anything that the official ballet composers could possibly hope to achieve. Understandably enough, Tschaikovsky was not enthusiastic about writing for ballet.

Petipa persuaded him to do so, in spite of the fact that he was known to be one ballet master who insisted on keeping control over the music and who gave a composer who had been commissioned to write a ballet very strict instructions on how

20

the score would have to be done in order to fit the ballet's story and steps. Somehow the two men managed to collaborate: some of the greatest classical ballets of all time resulted from that collaboration: *Swan Lake, The Nutcracker* and *Sleeping Beauty.*

In the greatest of the Russian nineteenth-century ballets, everything worked together: the music, the staging, the scenery, the costumes and the choreography. For the first time, dance became not just a spectacle or an entertainment to show the beauty and skill of a ballerina or the athletic ability and charm of a male dancer, but an integrated whole with all parts working together to intensify the total effect.

We do not have an exact record of how those Petipa ballets were actually danced. We have to get our impressions from descriptions written by authors and reporters of that time, plus paintings and lithographs. But even today choreographers work to try to recreate those marvelous Petipa ballets through these impressions, and through the human chain of dancers teaching roles to younger dancers that reaches through the barriers of time.

At the beginning of the twentieth century, ballet stages in Russia and in Europe were still anchored solidly in forms and stories made popular a hundred years earlier. Princes and princesses were whirling and twirling through romantic forest glens, often to a sad but picturesque death. The technique of the individual dancers had improved, but in staging, scene design and music very little had changed. Petipa's ballets still reigned supreme, and most new choreographies tended to be pale imitations of his *Swan Lake* and *Giselle.*

Meanwhile, writers, composers and painters were taking a very different view of the world around them. They were rapidly clearing the romantic haze away. Writers were exploring conflicts within the individual and between the individual and society. They dealt with problems of love and hate, good and evil in much more complex ways than had Romantic novelists and poets.

Composers were writing scores that were ragged, discordant and sometimes strident, but often immensely powerful, leaving behind them much of what had been harmonious and melodic in the nineteenth century. Painters were looking at their subjects with new eyes too, often distorting the human figure, the still life or the landscape in works of art that told us more about the subject and the painter than the photographic realism of an earlier age.

Serge Diaghilev arrived in St. Petersburg from his home town of Perm in 1890 to study law. He soon found that he was considerably less interested in his university studies than in the artistic life that swirled around him. By 1898, he had given up law entirely and had founded a magazine designed to bring the new art to the Russian public. Like many of his later ventures, the magazine was very influential but financially unprofitable. A year later, he took a job editing a journal for the Maryinski Theater, the ballet capital of the world, and his lifelong fascination with dance and dancers began.

He was, from the beginning, a difficult man, and he soon quarreled with the theater management and decided to take himself and his ideas to Paris, where he felt he might be received with more sympathy. He organized several concerts of Russian music there, and in 1908, brought a whole opera company from Russia. This created a sensation. The following year he decided to try his hand at managing a ballet, taking to Paris the best of the Maryinski dancers. Somehow he managed to persuade the Imperial Ballet to grant everybody leaves of absence.

In 1909, he opened a Paris season of ballet that was a triumph, and this determined the rest of his career. Among the dancers he brought from the Maryinski was a small, rather strange-looking young man with amazing technical ability and a strong sense of drama and music. His name was Vaslav Nijinsky —the first male dancer to become an international celebrity, and the one dancer to whom all other male dancers (often to their chagrin) have been compared over the decades.

Diaghilev saw the young dancer's possibilities immediately. He took him, along with Michel Fokine, a young choreographer, to Paris where he commissioned ballets with scenery and costumes by that city's outstanding painters and scores by the most revolutionary composers he could find. Just as the combination of Petipa and Tschaikovsky had electrified the ballet world in the previous century, now the combination of Diaghilev, Fokine and the composer Stravinsky created dance performances unlike any that had been seen before.

After several seasons, Diaghilev realized that borrowing dancers from the Maryinski when that company was not in season was not sufficient. He needed a permanent company of his own, built around Fokine as a choreographer and Nijinsky as a principal dancer and star attraction. Fokine managed to keep his position at the Imperial Ballet in spite of doing most of his work for Diaghilev's new company, headquartered in Monaco and called "The Ballet Russe de Monte Carlo." But Diaghilev clearly wanted Nijinsky dancing only for him. So he had to persuade the young dancer to forsake the security of the Imperial Ballet (where dancers not only were paid regular salaries, but also were given a pension at age thirty-five) and to throw his lot entirely with the Ballet Russe, in spite of its haphazard finances.

Fokine's ballets for Nijinsky and others were different from anything anyone had developed before. There were few evening-long spectacles. Most of his choreographies were relatively short, allowing three or more ballets to be performed in one evening. He used classical ballet steps and moves, but managed to transform them so that they corresponded to the subject matter, period and the character of the music. He used groups of dancers not just as ornaments or as background for the soloists but as part of the pattern of the total choreography. Most of all, every aspect of the dances was made to enhance all other aspects.

The roles Fokine created for Nijinsky somehow managed to capture the essential nature of this young dancer. He presented him as a strange, exotic character: the golden slave who seduces the Sultan's favorite harem girl, the sad half-human puppet Petrouchka, the ghostly specter of a rose.

No male dancer had ever been able to dance with such formidable technique. His jumps became legendary. So did his ability to transform himself into the character he was dancing.

The Specter of the Rose was, for its time, a rather strange ballet. It featured only two dancers: an anonymous girl who spent most of the dance apparently asleep in a chair and the specter who enters by the window and, from that second on, never stops moving. This is how Jean Cocteau, one of the great artists of his time, described the ballet with Nijinsky:

"In his costume of curling petals, behind which the girl perceives the image of her recent dancing partner, he comes through the blue cretonne curtains out of the warm June night. He conveys—which one would have thought impossible—the impression of some melancholy, imperious scent. Exulting in his rosy ecstasy, he seems to impregnate the muslin curtains and take possession of the dreaming girl. It is a most extraordinary achievement. By magic, he makes the girl dream she is dancing and conjures up all the delights of the ball."

Looking at the *Specter of the Rose* today, it is difficult to imagine why it caused such a sensation. Indeed it seems a rather artificial, sentimental little piece. The Nijinsky costume, a pink leotard covered with green rose leaves, looks strange on most male dancers.

Apparently, there was something in Nijinsky's personality that exactly suited that strange role and that nobody else has ever been able to capture since his time.

Another role, the puppet Petrouchka, has fared much better. This ballet is still danced by many companies today, not as a historical oddity but as an important part of regular repertory. It seems to be a particular favorite of Russian dancers who have left their country in search of more freedom, perhaps because the search for freedom is one of the themes of this psychologically complicated ballet. As one of the critics put it after Nijinsky's first performance: "The greatest difficulty of the Petrouchka part is to express his pitiful oppression and his hopeless efforts to achieve personal dignity without *ceasing to be a puppet. . . .*"

Petrouchka, to a wonderful, evocative score commissioned by Diaghilev from Stravinsky, may be the first ballet that had layers of meaning, that dealt with psychology and philosophy as well as telling a story.

The story is very simple. There is a street fair somewhere in Russia. Among the many attractions there are a dancing bear, a balloon seller and a puppeteer-magician, who displays three puppets, the sad clown Petrouchka, the dancing ballerina doll, and the physically strong but violent and insensitive blackamoor. The magician shows off his dolls. The crowd applauds. At this point the scene shifts, and we see Petrouchka being tossed by his master into a black cell, the prison where he apparently spends most of his time. He desperately tries to claw his way out. The ballerina doll, with whom he is in love, appears briefly, but leaves to visit the second cell, bright and garishly decorated, which belongs to the blackamoor. She and the blackamoor play and flirt. Petrouchka walks in and tries to take the ballerina away with him. The blackamoor attacks him. At that point, the scene shifts back to the street fair where performances are continuing. Suddenly Petrouchka appears, chased by the Moor with a sword. The

Moor kills him as the ballerina doll looks on. The crowd is stunned but relieved when the magician picks up the puppet and shows it is made only of straw. (Through a stage trick, the straw doll is substituted for the dancer.) The crowd leaves. At that point, Petrouchka appears on the roof of the puppet theater, exultant and apparently free. The magician looks at him in wonder and then leaves. As he leaves, the puppet collapses and dies.

Looking at pictures of Nijinsky as Petrouchka, it is evident that he *became* that doll-man. Under the sad make-up, it is almost impossible to recognize the face of the dancer. Other contemporary dancers use the same costume and the same make-up, but they do not seem to be able to entirely turn themselves into the character as Nijinsky was able to do. They *represent* Petrouchka. Nijinsky was apparently able to *become* Petrouchka, just as he would turn himself into the spirit of a rose.

Eventually, Diaghilev encouraged his young star dancer to make some ballets for himself. The most famous of these, and the one that has survived in the repertory of many modern companies, is *The Afternoon of a Faun* to the music of Debussy. In it Nijinsky used a new and completely revolutionary technique of dancing. He had looked at many of the Greek vases in museums throughout the world. On those vases he saw the flat, two-dimensional friezes of fauns and nymphs dancing. This is the picture he tried to achieve in his choreography. The ballet was almost entirely done in profile. The pace was slow. There were no leaps . . . only a sturdy progression of squared, rather than rounded movements. The whole ballet looked as if the fauns and nymphs had walked off one of those Greek friezes.

The story is also very simple. The faun lies on a rock eating grapes. He sees seven nymphs and his desire is aroused by one who undresses to bathe in the stream, but when he tries to approach her, she leaves and he has to console himself with the scarf she left behind. The faun releases his sexual tension while lying on the scarf.

When it was first performed, the ballet caused a scandal. For the first time the Diaghilev company and Nijinsky were booed, partly because of the sexually graphic ending (which today would not even shock the Moral Majority), but also because the dancers did not do what they were expected to do: in the opinion of the audience, a Nijinsky who did not leap and twirl was not dancing. Diaghilev, who believed in the ballet his protégé had made, but who also saw an opportunity for worldwide publicity, had the curtain rung down, and then immediately had the whole ballet repeated. The war that erupted between the detractors and defenders of the choreography in the press and in drawing rooms could only help to fill theaters wherever the ballet was performed, he felt. Of course, he was right. It was standing room only whenever the *Faun* was scheduled on the program.

But all the publicity surrounding Nijinsky as a choreographer began to annoy Fokine. After all, he had contributed dozens of successful ballets to the company. And yet all of Paris was talking about the first effort of this young dancer. Eventually, he fought with Diaghilev and left the company in anger.

Nijinsky never repeated his first popular success as a choreographer. The ballet he made to another Stravinsky score, *The Rite of Spring*, was almost universally condemned by critics and public alike.

What Nijinsky and Stravinsky were showing were the birth pangs of nature, the convulsions of the elements. Today, though the ballet by Nijinsky is rarely performed, the music has been used by other, modern choreographers in a variety of different ways.

Shortly after the disastrous opening, Nijinsky, not accompanied by Diaghilev (who apparently was deathly afraid of ocean travel), went by boat from France to South America. On the trip he married a member of the company's corps, a wealthy young Hungarian, Romola De Pulsky, who had been pursuing him for over a year. When Diaghilev heard of the marriage, he immediately fired Nijinsky in a jealous rage.

Without his mentor, Nijinsky's career declined rapidly. He tried to organize his own company and failed. Two years later he briefly rejoined the Diaghilev company and toured the United States with this group. The tour was not a success. Still in his twenties, Nijinsky settled in Switzerland with his wife. Symptoms of mental illness, which had appeared earlier but apparently had subsided, reappeared. He was hospitalized and remained in hospitals, severely mentally ill, until he died in 1953.

Diaghilev rehired Fokine for several more ballets. He also developed a new dancer and choreographer, Leonid Massine, who like Fokine and Nijinsky before him, had been a star dancer at the Imperial Ballet.

Diaghilev, in his later years, was to develop one other choreographer, possibly the greatest of all time: George Balanchine. He too had been a dancer with the Maryinski and joined Diaghilev's company as a dancer and later as a choreographer. His work is seen throughout the world today, and he founded the company that throughout the decades from the 1950s to the 1980s has brought the best of ballet to American audiences, the New York City Ballet.

Diaghilev died of diabetes in Venice in 1929. The last performance of his company was given at Covent Garden in London on July 26, 1929. It included two Balanchine ballets: *The Ball* and *The Prodigal Son.*

CHAPTER III

How Americans Began
to Dance

Every group of people that has lived on the American
continent, anthropologists tell us, even the suppos-
edly stoic Indians, has been restless and explosive in
expression. This shows the migration of entire peo-
ples, the moving about of individuals, as well as in
the tension and dynamics of dancing . . . in other
words, their pace.

AGNES DE MILLE, dancer, choreographer,
teacher and writer in *America Dances.*

THE INDIANS may have danced, but the Puritans didn't.
To the Indians, dancing developed skills needed for their very
survival: for hunting and fighting. Dance was also part of their
religious rituals. They danced when they wanted their gods to
give them rain. They also danced when they wanted the rain to
stop. Agnes de Mille tells us that one of their ritual dances, the
buffalo dance, lasted as long as nineteen days. "At the end of
which time, the young men in a state of semihypnosis believed

themselves to be buffalo, and so found it an easy matter to go out on the plains and call in the herd to be slaughtered."

If the Indians danced as part of their religion, the Puritans and other religious groups who first settled in this country did not as part of *theirs*. For many, there was no theater, not even any music except for hymns in church. Indeed, some of the strictest sects even forbade singing of sacred music or the playing of an instrument in their churches.

So it is no wonder that dancing in general, and ballet in particular, came to America as late as it did. While ballets were being performed in European courts, the dances Americans saw in the beginning were the folk dances brought over by Irish, Scottish and English newcomers who were not of the strict religious groups. Square dances and rounds had their origin in these countries. Dance historians tell us that in America square dances were probably performed much faster than in Europe, and that the individual sets were longer. "Americans were strong people who could stay through the course of an evening's dance after a day's plowing," says Agnes de Mille.

In the seventeenth century, these dances looked and sounded very much the way they look and sound today. Usually there was a fiddler playing country tunes, and a caller who called out what steps were to be performed by the couples.

By the time the nineteenth century arrived, the strict churches had lost their influence in wide areas. In ballrooms throughout America, elaborately dressed men and women were dancing the same steps that aristocrats all over Europe were dancing: minuets, gavottes and pavanes. These dances had elaborate patterns requiring complicated footwork. They were, however, much slower than the country dances.

There was one other difference between the country dances and the ballroom variety: in square dancing, partners swung each other around the floor, in ballroom men and women might delicately touch each other's fingertips, but there was no body contact. In both country and ballroom dancing, the rhythms were steady . . . no missed or irregular beats. One knew exactly what to expect next.

But another very different form of dancing was developing side-by-side with what the white folks did at the grange and in the ballroom. "In slave quarters, black men and women, brought over by the million from Africa to work in the fields and homes of their white owners, were doing dances they had learned in their native land. The rhythm was completely different from those European dance tunes that had been imported by the white settlers. They introduced syncopation: the missed beat, the accent slipped to an unexpected count. Often, as they watched black children dance on plantations, white children, realizing that these steps were a lot more fun than the carefully designed, slow dances they were taught by their dancing masters, copied the steps or even joined in the dance. A new kind of lilt took over the nation's songs and dances: the accent was placed not on the downbeat as in Europe, *one*-two, but on the upbeat or offbeat, one-*two*. This was African, but it became American," said Agnes de Mille.

If white music and dance were influenced by the black heritage, one form of dance, generally credited to blacks in America, actually had its roots in Irish and English folk dancing. Tap did not originate in the black community. It is an adaptation of clog dancing brought to this country by Irish and English immigrants in the eighteenth and nineteenth centuries.

Indeed American dance may be the one part of our lives that is truly the melting pot about which we have heard so much. While all kinds of experts are now telling us that our ethnic, national and racial backgrounds are not as easily melted down as had been supposed earlier, the best of dance did indeed, over 200 years, incorporate forms of movement and expression from almost every national and racial group that entered this country in large numbers.

Formal dance performances did not really come into this country until the middle of the nineteenth century, and no wonder. In the first place, to most Europeans, America looked like an uncharted wilderness. In the second place, the way to get here, by ship, was both perilous and uncomfortable. Even in those days, dancers must have felt the need to stay in training, and practicing ballet steps on a tossing, rocking ship must have seemed like a very difficult way to remain in shape.

America itself had no dance companies, although in 1833, an Italian immigrant, Lorenzo da Ponte, gave up his career as a storekeeper in Elizabeth, New Jersey, to bring troups of Italian singers and dancers to New York. European stars who were persuaded, usually by promises of a great deal of money, to journey across the Atlantic in the middle of the nineteenth century, usually returned home disappointed and told their colleagues that America was not worth the trip. They found, of course, that there were no trained groups of dancers with whom they could perform. If they did not wish to appear on stage by themselves, their managers had to collect, as quickly as possible, likely-looking men and women to whom they showed a few steps. The audiences, not accustomed to dance performances, either stayed away in droves or looked puzzled and unenthusiastic.

Not until 1840 did America accept enthusiastically its first imported star dancer. She was Fanny Elssler, who according to one of her biographers, came to America "out of pure greed." She was guaranteed $500 per performance, a huge sum in those days and, at those prices, she toured this country steadily for two years.

There was also a native partner for her. His name was George Washington Smith, an actor, who had studied dance. Before Elssler's arrival in this country, he had played bit parts in Shakespearean dramas and, occasionally, was asked to perform a hornpipe or some other popular dance between acts. But he had studied European dance styles with a French immigrant who had been a ballet master in Europe.

Elssler arrived here with a partner, James Sylvain (his real name was Sullivan and he was Irish). When she found that Smith was able to share the stage with her, she directed Sylvain to go out and recruit a company. Obviously, the untrained American dancers could not compare with their European counterparts. What's more, the costumes worn by company members were usually rented, rarely fitted, and sometimes were completely inappropriate for whatever was being danced. But American audiences had never seen anything like the Elssler performances, so went wild over the European dancer and the shows she was able to put together. In New York, a group of early balletomanes unhitched the horses from her carriage and pulled it through the streets, cheering. In Washington, the United States Congress was forced to recess every time she gave a performance: there were not enough senators and representatives on the floor of either house to constitute a quorum. Everybody was at the theater watching the fascinating young dancer from abroad.

Dance reviews and lithographs show us that the first native American dancer to try out some of the Elssler steps, as well as some of the great classic ballets, was Mary Ann Lee. She apparently was trained by George Washington Smith, who became a partnerless male dancer, and therefore completely unemployable, as soon as Elssler left for home. But mainly he reserved his skills to partner other European stars who made the trip across the Atlantic in hope of finding the streets as paved in gold coins as Elssler had found them.

Ballet really did not take root in the United States until the twentieth century. Eager managers imported European dancers including such stars as Anna Pavlova, who played to more or less enthusiastic houses. But the quality as well as the quantity of American ballet was poor, according to all reports written before and after the Civil War.

Meanwhile, however, we were developing our own form of dance spectacle, the New York musical, with its early corps of well-built, tall young women who paraded around the stage. Since these early chorus girls wore tights, rather than the long skirts that were still mandatory for women who were not on the stage, they were ogled eagerly by the men in the audience and generally condemned by the preachers in the churches. Also, they earned miserable salaries, so that they had to find ways to supplement the money they made on stage by a variety of other activities, which ranged from working as waitresses to other less desirable or less legal occupations.

One other form of dance would become popular in this country during the middle of the nineteenth century: the minstrel show. Eventually, it would turn into a mockery of black dance and life: a group of white male entertainers in black make-up, holding American blacks up to ridicule. But the first great minstrel star was black himself. He called himself Juba (his real name was William Henry Lane), and he invented his own steps and danced them to syncopated music. One of the characters he danced regularly was called "Jim Crow"—that is where the term for discrimination against American blacks originated. But, according to no less a critic than Charles Dickens, he was a great star who brought down the house regularly with his combination of fast footwork, high jumps, and snapping fingers. He even toured Europe where the new style of "American" dance was greatly admired.

America's first genuine ballerina, Augusta Maywood, tried dancing in America but found it unprofitable and artistically disappointing. She went to Europe and became a star at the Paris

Opera Ballet. Important choreographies were written for her there, but she did not perform them in her native country since no one wanted to pay to see her. Eventually, she settled in Italy where she died never having performed even once in a major opera house or theater in this country.

So, after Fanny Elssler, dance in general (with some exceptions), and ballet in particular, was on a steady downward course in the United States until the turn of the century when an American dancer, Isadora Duncan, set out to revolutionize dance styles not only in this country but in Europe as well.

CHAPTER IV

Isadora Duncan and Other Rebels

Isadora bared the limbs so that we might see not so much the naked body, but revealed emotion. She rediscovered spontaneity and individual passion. She did to her art what Luther did to the medieval church. She questioned it.

—AGNES DE MILLE IN *America Dances*

I SADORA DUNCAN was born in San Francisco and died in Nice on the French Riviera, in 1927. Her dancing career was relatively short, her artistic ability questionable, and her methods of persuasion often humorless and strident. But working entirely by herself, with no company, no patron and no money to back her, she changed the face of dance throughout the world for all time.

As a young girl in California she started ballet lessons. But for a variety of reasons (including the fact that she simply did not have the body of a ballerina), she found the strict techniques too confining. Ballet toe shoes reminded her of the bound feet of Chinese women, she often said. Ballet class was boring, repetitive and dictatorial, she felt. Story ballets were silly and sense-less, she pointed out. So she invented her own system of dance, based on her own abilities, convictions and prejudices.

She got rid of costumes, corsets and footwear. Her dance dress was a loose, Grecian-style dress; her legs and feet were bare.

But she revolutionized dance in ways that went beyond the fact that she refused to use classical steps and technique, or wear the accepted dress of the ballerina. She took her art seriously—deadly seriously it seems, when one reads her intense and earnest autobiography. At a time when in America dance was at best a diversion, she made it respectable as an art form.

Her technique was a kind of emotional movement to music, not based on ballet positions or formalized techniques. Her dances did not tell stories; instead they gave an interpretation of the music to which she danced. She did not use traditional ballet music either. Her performances were accompanied by Beethoven symphonies, Schubert concertos and Chopin waltzes.

All her movements were based on the way humans move normally. She frequently indicated that if nature had meant us to dance on one toe, she would have arranged for our feet to be built differently. She also scorned such "acrobatic tricks" as high jumps and fast turns. Although photography had been discovered by the time Isadora Duncan performed, film was still in its infancy. We only have a few snatches of her late choreography on film, which gives us merely an idea of how she moved. Some of her pupils are also still alive today, and they can show us what kinds of dances she performed. But her principal message came through in her book: "Anybody can and should dance . . . it's good for the body and the spirit."

Her first attempt at giving performances in San Francisco and New York were not successful. She was attempting to interest Americans, who were not even particularly taken with ballet, in a revolt against this art form. But in Europe, ballet had thousands of avid followers. And it was in Europe that Duncan's revolt against ballet took root.

In her tunic, veils and bare feet, she danced in Paris, Budapest, Berlin and Beirut, and wherever she went, other women who had never thought of dancing before discarded corsets, shoes and stockings and danced after her.

She went to Russia in 1905, and her new ideas impressed and probably influenced no less than Michel Fokine. What he apparently admired was not her technique, or lack of it. Instead he was interested in her ability to use many different kinds of music, and to perform dances that did not portray a complicated story.

While Duncan herself fascinated many of her audiences, those who chose to follow in her bare footsteps often did not. She started schools in several cities, including Moscow, and eager mothers sent their little daughters to study with her. The children, according to some of the literature of those days, apparently had a wonderful time, but few of them became professional dancers and none reached the kind of prominence that Duncan herself enjoyed for a time.

Duncan's problem was a basic one. She wanted to throw out artificiality, pomp and pretense in dance. She did so, but along with these qualities, also threw out discipline and technique. She felt that dance should express the dancer's emotions, and apparently was talented enough to make that expression interesting to an audience. But many of her pupils were not so talented.

But, although her specific choreographies were not preserved, her spirit influenced other dancers to develop a style and form of their own. In many ways she is the mother of *modern* dance in both Europe and America, and her views made an enormous impression on *ballet* choreographers as well.

Duncan held radical beliefs on other aspects of life as well as dance. She had strong views on marriage (she was against it), sex (it should be free), rearing of children (not too much discipline, lots of love and freedom), clothes (nothing should confine the body). What's more, she insisted on living her life by her precepts.

In the end she was exhausted, lonely and broke. She drank too much and picked up too many young men. Her death was, in a way, much like her life. One evening in Nice she got into an open convertible with a man she had just met. "Goodbye my friends," she said in French. "I am going to glory." Her long scarf caught in one of the wheels of the car, and she was strangled accidentally.

In spite of the fact that her schools had not developed any individual dancers of note, this thoroughly untraditional woman left a tradition behind her. Many of the young girls who had been her pupils worked to develop their own approach to dance. She had also, for the first time, indicated that a woman could have her own company without a male manager or even a partner. Among the women inspired by her was Ruth St. Denis.

Ruth St. Denis, born in 1877, began dancing only a few years after Duncan. She too discarded toe shoes, right along with most other ballet steps and traditions. Her particular kind of dance was influenced by Oriental dances. St. Denis had never been in the Orient when she first decided that this was the style that interested her most. In fact, her original inspiration came from a picture she saw on a brand of Egyptian cigarettes. But, over the years, she made an effort to meet as many Indians, Egyptians and men and women from other countries whose dances she wished to adapt, and she really did learn a great deal about their native art forms.

She did not use Oriental music. Like Duncan, she picked the composers whose works she loved for her choreographies. Unlike Duncan, she often used elaborate costumes.

She had some success in the United States but won her greatest early acclaim in Europe. When St. Denis returned to the United States with a small company of dancers she had trained herself, she went on a coast-to-coast tour. She was a critical success, but a financial failure. She also performed in vaudeville, where audiences, used to "Oriental" dancers with bare bellies rotating their hips to fake Turkish or Egyptian tunes, must have been a little surprised at what they saw.

In 1914, she met a theology student turned dancer, Ted Shawn, who became her partner. They married and formed a company and school called Denishawn, where modern dance was taught along with related arts, such as music and philosophy. This was the first serious school of dance in the United States meant not just for young girls whose mothers wished them to improve their posture but for potentially professional artists. Ted Shawn also projected the kind of masculine image that allowed him to attract young boys as well as girls into dance. For decades American boys had been discouraged from dancing professionally because their parents felt that somehow dance was unmasculine. Many Americans still feel that way in spite of the fact that a male dancer, whether in ballet or modern dance, has to have the strength, agility and skill of a baseball player, boxer or high jumper.

But even with the school and continuous touring through this country, St. Denis and Shawn found that they could not support themselves. Repeatedly, they did what Duncan had always refused to do: they appeared in vaudeville and, eventually, in one of the stylish and highly popular Broadway extravaganzas, the *Ziegfeld Follies.* Apparently both felt that entertainment and art need not conflict. Duncan scorned any popular American art form, which may be one of the reasons she died deeply in debt. St. Denis and Shawn managed to keep their school going, trained many well-known modern dancers, and paid their bills on time.

Their choreographies, however, are no longer part of modern dance repertory. If they are done at all, they are performed by their students as a tribute to their great teachers, or for historical interest.

After Ruth St. Denis, a number of lesser-known and less gifted dancers used her Oriental themes, but none was as successful.

What had happened by now, however, was that in America, dance was accepted as part of musical theater. Entertainment, which was supposed to be fun, and culture, which was supposed to be good for you but dull, had been combined. Over the decades, dance in America would develop in several directions, but the two main ones had already emerged by the end of World War I: ballet, using the techniques formalized in Europe by Petipa, of early interest to only a few; and modern dance, based on Duncan, St. Denis and Shawn, of wider interest. Eventually choreographers would find ways to mix these styles in dance companies, on the musical stage, and in films.

CHAPTER V

Dance in America: Broadway and Films

The chorus dancing at the turn of the century was still parades of pretty girls and pseudo-handsome men who escorted them off and on stage. They could sing well enough to back up solo parts. Dancing was not required. The ambition of the girls was to marry wealth. The ambition of the boys was hard to define. The purpose on stage of both was to show off costumes and to provide relief and diversion from the book.

—AGNES DE MILLE in *America Dances*

WHILE BALLET in Europe was growing and developing, no companies were formed in the United States and no schools were started to train native soloists. In fact, even the Broadway stage, at the turn of the century, had few dancers. Anyone who wished to see dance had to go to a local hotel, where one might take a few turns around the floor during the tea hour; or if one lived in a rural area, one might attend the church social or the annual country fair where, as part of the festivities, there might be a dance of some sort. Americans danced as part of a social occasion. They rarely watched others dance, either as an art or entertainment.

Occasionally, between 1910 and 1920, an enterprising manager would bring a star dancer and company over from Europe for performances in major American cities.

Anna Pavlova, one of the great ballerinas of all time, was brought here by Sol Hurok, whose eye for potentially popular entertainment was excellent, but who had no interest in developing dancers or dance companies in this country. Pavlova was a huge success. She toured the country several times, wore herself out in the process and, according to those who knew her, made enough money to retire. She was, apparently, brilliant. Again, one has to use the reviewers of her time and the still photographs of her performances to judge the quality of her dancing. Her company was made up mainly of a group of young women, and a few men who came more with adventurous spirits and a desire for regular employment than training or talent for ballet.

By 1929, a theater owner, S. L. "Roxy" Rothafel, decided that New Yorkers might be ready for a regular series of ballets. He brought Leonid Massine, Diaghilev's brilliant choreographer, to this country to mount a series of performances with a resident company made up, in part, of American dancers at the Roxy Theater, near New York City's Times Square. Massine, who was accustomed to being taken seriously as an artist, found that he was supposed to put on a new program every ten days or so . . . right along with the trained seals, jugglers and comedians that made up the rest of the Roxy variety program. After one year he left and presumably told his European colleagues that as far as dance was concerned, Americans were a group of hopeless barbarians.

Meanwhile, musical theater in New York had begun to change. There were still a lot of shows billed as "Follies" or "Scandals" that featured tall, long-legged girls in exceedingly elaborate costumes parading around the stage. Show girls needed to be tall and thin, have good legs, reasonably good posture and, one hoped, pretty faces. They did not need to be dancers. There was and had been some dancing in musical plays known as operettas. And, of course, the opera had always had dancing of a sort. But dancing as a really important part of anything was lacking.

Then, here and there a producer began mounting what became known as a "review" or as just a plain "musical." In these productions, the principals and even those in minor roles needed dancing skills. These dances were not based on European ballet or even on the kind of experimentation done by American modern dancers like Isadora Duncan. What was beginning to happen in musical plays on Broadway was an adaptation of an English-Irish art form that blacks in America had made their own: tap. While in Europe boys and girls who wanted to dance were going to ballet classes; in America youngsters were taking tap, either for fun or with a view of making it on the Broadway stage.

But before dance became really important to Broadway theater, it had already become the main ingredient in many films.

The note by a talent scout that accompanied Fred Astaire's first screen test may indeed have said: "Can't act; can't sing; slightly bald; can dance a little," but somehow the story seems unlikely. Whatever the scout may have thought of Astaire's acting, singing and hairline, there was never any doubt that he could dance . . . and dance like no one else had ever danced before him.

Astaire's dancing really cannot be described by any adjectives that might have been used before he made his first film. It combined the best of tap (seen previously only in top form in black dance acts), some ballet techniques and something that, for lack of a better term, one might call theater dancing. To the average moviegoer, Astaire was not primarily a dancer: he was a movie star. What he did seemed easy, a part of the character he played on the screen. The character was always essentially the same: an average American Joe, wearing a top hat and tails to please a snooty girl or employer or some other person, not himself. He looked as if his natural form of dress might be a pair of slacks and a shirt open at the throat (blue jeans in those days were only worn by cowboys). He combined folksiness with elegance, and his dances looked easy and spontaneous, as if he could just stop walking and start dancing, without rehearsal or even without thought.

Of course, nothing could have been less true. The dances were made for him by a master choreographer with the unlikely name of Hermes Pan, and they took days and sometimes weeks of rehearsal. His costars, including Ginger Rogers, noted that they often danced until their feet bled, and they still had to shoot a sequence over and over, because the apparently easygoing

Astaire was a master craftsman and a perfectionist. He was also America's first superdancer in every sense of the word.

After Astaire came Gene Kelly, a very different kind of dancer. With Kelly, one was much more conscious of dance as separate from the dancer. Compared to Astaire's easygoing personality and apparently spontaneous movements, Kelly's dances *looked* as carefully choreographed as they were. One is also aware, watching him do a solo turn in *Singin' in the Rain* or *An American in Paris,* how difficult those fast steps and high jumps he is showing us are. Kelly looks like a dancer who sometimes acts.

In any case, Americans who had apparently considered ballet and even modern dance as something exotic, peculiar and somehow not suitable for this country, simply accepted dancing in the movies as part of the entertainment they enjoyed. Why movie dancing was looked upon differently from dancing on the ballet stage is not quite clear, except that, partly because of the Diaghilev-Nijinsky legends about aristocratic patronage, homosexuality and other traits with which the average American could not identify, ballet dancers, especially male ballet dancers, were still seen as strange. Certainly a mother whose son might announce that he wanted to join a European ballet company would probably have been more than a little upset. On the other hand, if Johnny had told her he was planning to go to Hollywood to become the second Fred Astaire or Gene Kelly, she might have considered him somewhat unrealistic, but not in any way peculiar.

Dance came to Broadway stage later than it did to films. There had been revues and other shows that featured tap dancers, usually black men and women. There had also been those scandals and follies that featured a row of long-legged non-dancing chorus girls. There were the so-called operettas in which the principals sang, the chorus sometimes joined them, and occasionally, someone either danced a waltz or a polka. But the performers who were called upon to do a few dance steps were actors and singers who had, as part of their training, learned a little about dancing.

Then, in 1935, a musical opened on Broaday called *I Married an Angel.* It had as its principal star a ballerina, Vera Zorina, from the post-Diaghilev Ballet Russe de Monte Carlo. What is even more important, it had as its choreographer the last of the greatest of several choreographers Diaghilev had discovered and nurtured: George Balanchine.

I Married an Angel contained two ballets that were an integral part of the story. Although nobody noticed it much at the time, the story itself had elements of nineteenth century elves, enchanted princesses and other similar creatures in it. Zorina played an angel (rather than an enchanted swan) who falls in love with a mortal. Unlike those romantic nineteenth century classics, there was, of course, a happy ending. There was also a great score by Richard Rogers with words by Lorenz Hart. But, most of all, there were real dancers trained in ballet and brought into the show by Balanchine.

Balanchine had attempted to bring ballet to America and had not succeeded. The time was not right. So he turned to the musical stage. After *Angel* another show, *On Your Toes*, had an equally brilliant, innovative choreography. It starred, along with another ballerina from the Ballet Russe, Tamara Geva, Ray Bolger, a very American dancer in the Astaire style. Somehow, Balanchine was able to combine classical techniques with American forms of dance. Both of the musicals were exceedingly successful. Critics loved them and so did the public. And what they loved most was the dancing.

Later Balanchine's dances helped to turn a show that might easily have looked like just one more picturesque operetta, *Song of Norway*, into a totally different experience. Again, he used dancers trained by the Ballet Russe de Monte Carlo.

Balanchine also choreographed a Hollywood film, *The Goldwyn Follies*, which was very different from all the Follies that had preceded it. No more nondancing ladies in heavy costumes parading around, moving less than some of the scenery around them. No more smiling young men occasionally shaking a leg. Balanchine took his highly-trained group of accomplished young dancers with him from the ballet and Broadway, and the motion picture became essentially a dance showpiece.

Although the Broadway show and the film were both critical and popular successes, Balanchine apparently felt that, by his standards, they were not first-rate. As soon as he was able to find funds for a school of ballet and a permanent ballet company, he devoted himself exclusively to them, and never again choreographed, either for Broadway or for films.

Another choreographer, who would eventually create dances for ballet, also enjoyed her first success on Broadway. Agnes de Mille, the niece of Cecil B. de Mille, director and producer of Hollywood epics, had decided to become a classical dancer, but she was not a success in that capacity. Nor did her first serious dance work attract much attention. But with the Broadway show *Oklahoma*, which opened in 1943, she helped change the whole concept of musical theater in the United States. In that musical, dance is not a separate element—it is an integral part of the whole concept. De Mille uses dances not just to give characters something to do in order to flesh out a rather simple story, nor even to forward the action. In *Oklahoma*, the dancers are used to show a whole other side of the main characters, to give an indication of their fantasies, their fears and their inner lives. Because the dances are too demanding for singer-actors, the principal characters are played by two separate performers. There is a singing Laurie and a dancing Laurie, a singing Curley and a dancing Curley, a singing Judd Fry and a dancing Judd Fry.

Dancer-choreographer Murray Louis sums up in his book, *Inside Dance*, the powerful and lasting influence of Agnes de Mille. "What finally brought the two factions [ballet and modern dance] smack into each other was a third form of dance and the dancers themselves," he wrote. "It was a catalyst more powerful than Hollywood, more magnetic than the Met [the Metropolitan Opera in New York, which had, off and on, a not very good dance company]. It was Broadway, and it was engineered by a loner, Agnes de Mille. She was a loner in her vision and in her art, in her motivations and in her intelligence . . . After de Mille's *Oklahoma* opened on Broadway, and its success was ensured, all dance barriers came down. Show dancing, later to be called 'jazz' joined ballet and modern dance to become a huge melting pot, serving up whatever Broadway shows might need."

The success of her work in *Oklahoma* and other Broadway musicals made it possible for de Mille to choreograph for ballet when ballet companies finally found their place in the American artistic world.

Another dancer-choreographer, Jerome Robbins, started with a ballet *Fancy Free*, which is about three sailors on furlough in New York, and he eventually expanded that ballet into a musical comedy *On the Town*. From the beginning, original ballets in America were closely interwoven with what had happened in film and on the Broadway stage. Out of this mix, a new and unique art form was to develop, an interweaving of what had been best in the Hollywood and Broadway dances with what had been learned from Petipa and Diaghilev.

Although there was no successful, lasting ballet company in the United States until 1939, dance in general and ballet in particular gradually found acceptance because of what had happened during the nineteen-thirties and early forties on the New York stage and in Hollywood films. American choreographers and American dancers would never look quite like their European predecessors or even their present-day European colleagues. Without a long-standing tradition of classical ballet, America had created its own dance styles and forms, a melting pot of popular taste and great art.

CHAPTER VI

The Dance Explosion

No one imagined that Americans could dance; danc-
ing was for the Italians; dancing was for the Russians;
dancing was for the French. People who spoke English
did not dance. . . .

— Clive Barnes in *Contemporary Dance*

CLIVE BARNES, a noted dance reviewer who started working in England but has, for many decades, published mainly in the United States, thinks that American dance really started with Isadora Duncan. "She was totally free; she was inventing a vocabulary," he writes in his introduction to the book, *Contemporary Dance*. Her choreographies, he feels, were "a vision of America dancing. What was particularly American about it?" he asks. "I would say that it was a gesture of freedom. It was the first realization of space in dance. The interesting reason why American dance and Russian dance have something in common is that both originated in countries that are enormous in area. They came from countries where people have a large concept of movement, a large concept of space, a large concept of where things can move, where things can originate."

Certain kinds of American dance may indeed have been influenced by Isadora Duncan. But other kinds of dancing were influenced more by other factors: by Petipa at the French and Russian courts, by Diaghilev's brilliant dancers and choreographers, by British jigs and black tap, by Scottish rounds and Jewish horas, by Viennese waltzes and Polish mazurkas. American dance is a true melting pot of themes, origins, choreographers, even of dancers. Somehow we were able to attract the best from everywhere, and when the best got together, the dance explosion occurred.

The signs of that explosion are all around us today. Large national ballet companies have come into being and dance to critical acclaim and manage somehow to pay their bills. Small regional dance companies exist all over the United States, some excellent, some mediocre, but very few downright bad. Inferior dance companies usually survive for only a few seasons. Mediocre ones may survive five years or so if they can attract a few rich patrons. But many dance companies have survived for decades, and almost all of them are very good by any standard one cares to apply.

In Hartford, Connecticut, for instance, manager-choreographer Michael Utoff has put together a group of young men and women ballet dancers who give performances in many parts of the country. They dance some of the most difficult choreographies, and Utoff himself has made dances for them that look as interesting as anything one sees in some of the publicly-financed, internationally-known dance companies in Europe. In fact, his version of *Romeo and Juliet* to the Prokofiev score probably comes closest to Shakespeare's meaning of tragedy: unreasoning hatred hurts most of all the young, than any of the many other dance versions of that play. The company runs its own school, and its graduates find work in Europe as well as in the United States. And all of this happens on a budget that would make the manager of a state-supported dance company anywhere else in the world close up shop in despair.

There is a dance company in Utah with choreographers that use Western themes; one in San Francisco that has two resident choreographers who manage to produce ballets that look like Broadway shows (one of the two has recently choreographed Broadway's hit musical *Sophisticated Ladies*); a company in Dayton, Ohio, that is planning to use a work by a native son and New York City Ballet dancer, Joseph Duell, as part of its program; a company in Boston that was the first group of ballet dancers invited to China; and one in Philadelphia that manages to dance the most difficult works of American and European choreographers in superb style. When the magazine *Ballet News*, in about ten pages every month, lists the performances and programs of dozens of companies throughout the United States in a given week, there are always plaintive letters in the next issue about the ten, or twenty, or thirty companies that were left out.

Besides regional ballet companies, there are also ethnic ones. There is a Puerto Rican group in New York City, a Mexican-American one in a small town outside of Albuquerque, and best of all, the Dance Theater of Harlem, which, although started as a show piece for black dancers, has become one of the world's outstanding companies without any reference to skin color.

When Arthur Mitchell, a principal dancer with the New York City Ballet, decided to form a company in the Harlem community after Martin Luther King was assassinated, he was, perhaps, thinking more of the contribution dance could make to the pride and welfare of Harlem than of creating a major new dance organization that would rival much older and much more established companies. And, without the dance explosion in America, without the interest in dance and some of the financing that has become available through foundations, the New York State Council for the Arts and the National Endowment for the Arts, the company would probably not have become a reality, or at least not the major force in dance that it is today. Balanchine helped. He provided technical assistance and gave the company some of his finest works to perform. But that alone would not have been enough. Nor would the financial and moral support of the black community. The money and the interest had to come from many parts of the United States and from many sources, and it did.

The Dance Theater of Harlem has its own school. Until the winter of 1981, any youngster who wished to go to class was allowed to do so. Then, with deep cuts in the federal budget for the arts, the Dance Theater of Harlem, which had just returned from a world tour in which they had received the highest critical acclaim everywhere, found itself with very little money to continue those classes, or even the company.

The budget cuts that restricted the number of students the school could absorb have to be counted among the most shortsighted and heartless of the many funding cuts to the arts in 1982. Boys and girls who take regular dance class develop mental and physical discipline that will be invaluable to them in later life. They are usually healthy, physically and emotionally. Few drink, smoke or take drugs. Alcohol, cigarettes and uppers and downers just don't mix with ballet. The Dance Theater of Harlem was an important source of pride and health in this community.

Among the boys and girls who took class just because they thought it was fun, or for exercise, or to relieve boredom, tension and frustration, there were always a few who had the drive, the patience and the talent to make it as top professional dancers. The Harlem company has, in the past few years, produced some of the best ballet dancers in the world. The men are so good that they have been hired by the most prestigious companies in the United States. In 1980, Baryshnikov recruited one of the top male Harlem dancers for the American Ballet Theater, and gave him, for his solo debut, the male lead in the Balanchine choreography of Tschaikovsky's *Theme and Variations*. No other dancer in the company, with the exception of Baryshnikov himself, had danced that piece as well as Ronald Perry did.

In the winter of 1981, Mel Tomlinson, also of the Dance Theater of Harlem, joined the New York City Ballet. His debut was in a ballet choreographed by Balanchine for the founder of Tomlinson's former company, Arthur Mitchell. Tomlinson's spectacular performance in *Agon* was hailed by the *New York Times* as "electrifying." It also referred to his partner, Heather Watts (a New York City Ballet trained dancer), as "sensational" and to the entire production as "unforgettable." Those are words that are rarely used by dance critics. Both Tomlinson and Watts are able to do what they do because of the new prestige and new money that has gone into dance within the past decade. Watts came to the New York City Ballet from California via a Ford Foundation scholarship to the School of American Ballet; and Tomlinson from the School of the Dance Theater of Harlem, plus several years of intensive work in that company.

Somehow, no matter how many of the Harlem dancers are hired by larger companies that can pay better and offer a longer performance season, there always seem to be new and younger dancers to take their places. Probably, only financial bankruptcy would change that situation.

Besides the hundreds of ballet companies, there are also in-numerable companies that perform in a variety of dance tech-niques, usually grouped somewhat inaccurately under the term "modern." After all there are many *ballets* just as unlike *Swan Lake* as any work that "modern dance" has to offer. Perhaps a better way to describe the nonballet groups is to indicate that the women don't wear toe shoes and none of the dancers use standard ballet positions.

The best known of these dance groups perform all over the United States and the world. Their techniques and the type of choreographies they perform can often seem quite traditional. Martha Graham's dances, for instance, often tell stories, al-though these stories are exceedingly complicated and deal with deep emotional problems, unlike the simple fairy tales of the Romantic era. On the other hand, there are groups that seem to stage happenings rather than evenings or afternoons of dance. A modern choreographer, Meredith Monk, once commandeered a huge New York museum, the Guggenheim, and spread her danc-ers throughout the whole space, with the audience looking up from the first floor.* That performance included a dancer on a white horse, *outside* the museum. That was just the first week. The second week she took another part of the same choreography to the Barnard College Theater. The third section was given in a loft with none of the performers there. They appeared on video tape. The whole work was called *Juice*.

Then there was a choreography called *Roof Piece* by Patricia Brown that was actually performed on a series of roofs, covering an eleven block area in midtown New York. In another choreog-raphy she had her dancers walking on the walls of New York City's Whitney Museum. This was accomplished by rigging tracks along the ceiling, one track for each dancer, and putting the dancers in brown harnesses attached to pulleys and ropes. Since the pulleys and ropes were the same color as the dancers' costumes, and were therefore, almost invisible, those who saw the performance were under the illusion that the dancers were walking up the walls. One choreographer presented an evening

* (The inside of the building is one large, round, open space with a continuous ramp attached to the inside wall going to the top of the building.)

50

of dance in which he simply showed a blank stage with nothing or no one on it—a sort of nondance.

But most modern dance companies are more conservative. They use conventional stages, costumes and music. Their dances may even look a good deal like ballet. Or they may resemble a dance in a Broadway show. Or they may look like some kind of dance one has not seen before.

Broadway, the movies and television have become, of course, also part of the dance explosion. On Broadway in January of 1982, there were three shows dealing specifically with dance and dancers. One, *42nd Street,* featuring jazz and tap, had been a hit for two years. It had been adapted from a dance film of the 1930s, and told the often-repeated tale of the new, grass-green kid from the country who comes to New York to be a dancer. She somehow manages to get herself into the chorus of a show; the principal dancer is injured and, within one evening, Little Miss Nobody is the toast of the town. As anyone can see, *42nd Street* made it on the strength of its choreography and the skill of its dancers, not on the realism or intelligence of its story.

Another Broadway hit that has been playing for years, *A Chorus Line,* tells a much more realistic tale. Set as a Broadway audition, the director asks all the potential members of his corps to tell their stories. They do. Most of them are no longer the optimistic, wide-eyed youngsters of *42nd Street.* The first musical number in the show gives the theme, "I Need This Job . . . My God, I Need This Job." The professional and personal lives of the dancers are bleak indeed. Even the ones who are finally picked for the corps turn out to be included only as part of an anonymous line. One knows that come next month, they will probably be auditioning for another show. This, incidentally, is an excellent play to see if one has illusions about the glamorous life of Broadway gypsies (that's what professionals call Broadway dancers who play one show until it closes and then go on to another), in particular, or in dance in general.

A third musical just called *Dancin'* is exactly what the name implies: a series of dances by Broadway choreographer Bob Fosse. No story at all. Just a number of dances ranging from almost-ballet to modern jazz.

Among recent dance films *The Turning Point* and *All That Jazz* were box-office hits. *Nijinsky* was not, but was still seen by several hundred thousand people. There are frequent dance programs on public television, and the great old dance films of the Fred Astaire and Gene Kelly era are still on one of the late-late shows several times a week.

The dance explosion is with us. Those of us who love dance hope it stays . . . to become a habit, rather than a temporary fad.

CHAPTER VII

All Those Nutcrackers or The Problem Is Money

"Even before the curtain goes up," says Michael Smuin, codirector of the San Francisco Ballet, "we have half a million in advance sales at the box office. And David McLain, artistic director of the Cincinnati Ballet, admits that "We have survived as a company because of The Nutcracker.*"*

—*The New York Times,* Sunday, November 29, 1981

I N THE 1981 federal budget, the National Endowment for the Arts, which helps to support all arts—theater, music, writing, experimental films, as well as dance—was cut by one-third, to leave a total of about eighty-five million dollars. At the same time, the budget for military bands alone *was raised* to ninety-five million dollars, as part of the Pentagon allocation. In 1982, the American taxpayers paid more for the support of military bands, which rarely play for the public (and usually don't play very well at any time), than they did to help support all the arts throughout the United States.

53

Obviously, this means more fund-raising all around.

There are many ways in which dance companies raise money. The one thing they can't depend on for their operating budgets is ticket sales. Even completely sold-out houses don't pay for the cost of the performances for which those seats are sold. The New York City Ballet plays to a sold-out house throughout its American seasons: in New York, at Saratoga Springs and in other cities in which the company dances. If the company had to count on ticket sales alone, it would have been in the red for decades. And ticket sales certainly don't pay for the School of American Ballet, which has a large Ford Foundation grant for scholarships and has to find other ways to raise enough money to stay in business.

The American Ballet Theater has an even more serious problem. Its headquarters is the Metropolitan Opera in New York, a much larger house than the New York State Theater where the New York City Ballet dances. Ticket prices there are much higher. (In 1982, the top price for a City Ballet ticket was twenty-two dollars; for an American Ballet Theater ticket, the top was fifty dollars.) But because of the high prices the house sells out only for very popular performances: for instance, when Baryshnikov is dancing. For other performances the cheaper seats may be filled, but there are often noticeable gaps in the enormous orchestra section.

The Joffrey Ballet, another national company, has a short season at the City Center Theater in New York and travels some of the time. The problem with that theater is that it is very difficult to see the stage from many of the seats. Those who go to ballet regularly know where the sections are with the poor view, and since they cost just as much as the seats with adequate views, many regular patrons avoid them. So, large sections of that theater are often empty.

Add to this the fact that, just like the New York City Ballet, neither the American Ballet Theater nor the Joffrey can support itself on ticket sales alone, even if they played to standing room only every night, and the financial picture for ballet companies is bleak indeed. Most have counted on some government support through the National Endowment and through State councils for the arts.

There was a time when many people thought that supporting the arts with any kind of public money was somehow un-American, or even Communistic. The fact is, of course, that in almost every other Western country—in Canada, New Zealand, Australia, as well as in England, France, Germany (West and East), Denmark, Holland, and even supercapitalistic little Switzerland —the arts are almost *entirely* supported by government funds.

In Germany, England, Denmark and many other countries, dancers in national ballet companies are civil servants, just like members of the cabinet, or letter carriers for the Post Office. They get regular salaries year-round. What's more, when they are too old to dance or when they are injured, they get pensions— often their full salaries for the rest of their lives. They get free life insurance, free health insurance, and regular paid vacations, just like all other workers. American artists in general, and dancers in particular, get none of these benefits. There are few companies that have even a minimal pension plan or that provide their dancers with health insurance. None provides vacation pay. When the company is not dancing, the dancers receive unemployment insurance. If they are injured, they may get workman's compensation for a while but, unless they are truly unable to perform any other job because the injury has been totally disabling, they are eventually on their own and have to seek a new way of making a living. Since salaries at best are not very high, few can save for the years in which they won't be able to dance any longer. Cutting their pay more to make up for the money the United States government has taken away from dance, and turned over to already generously-endowed military bands, is out of the question. Most dancers can barely survive on what they earn as it is.

So the solution is to find the money elsewhere. There are some foundations that are particularly interested in the arts. There are gala performances, often with parties, balls or dinners after a special performance with ticket prices that can range from fifty dollars per seat up to several thousand, depending on what dance company is giving the gala and which celebrities promise to show up for the after-performance event.

Some dancers with a special following will, occasionally, dance a benefit for a company they feel deserves support. Baryshnikov has given benefits for a great many small, financially weak, but artistically strong, companies. Peter Martins helped the Hartford Ballet out of a severe money crunch by agreeing to dance Romeo in the first performance of Utoff's *Romeo and Juliet.*

Suzanne Farrell, Patricia McBride and other superdancers will donate their talents and their names to rescue faltering small dance companies. Top choreographers will, sometimes, make a special dance piece for a company that needs money to stay alive for another year.

But always, every year, there are all those *Nutcrackers.* In spite of higher-priced tickets for *Nutcracker* performances than for other performances, they sell out large opera houses, convention centers and hockey arenas wherever they are given in the United States. For some reason, the *Nutcracker,* an essentially European ballet, has never enjoyed the popularity in Europe that it does here. But here it helps keep innumerable ballet companies in the black.

It tells the story of a little girl (sometimes she is called Clara and sometimes Marie) who, at a Christmas party in her parents' house, is given a Nutcracker doll by a mysterious-looking friend or relative called Drosselmeyer. In some versions, Drosselmeyer brings along a little boy (a nephew, perhaps). At the end of the party Marie (or Clara) falls asleep and dreams. First she has a nightmare: the room has been invaded by a giant band of mice, led by the Mouse King, apparently out to cause some dreadful kind of mischief. To the rescue comes the Nutcracker, grown to man- or boy-size (depending on whose version you are seeing). He and a band of toy soldiers (also grown to human size) defeat the mice. The Nutcracker kills the Mouse King, sometimes with the help of Marie (Clara), who throws her slipper at his head.

At that point, the Nutcracker doll either turns into a little boy (the one Drosselmeyer brought to the party) or the prince, again depending on which version is being presented. He leads the little girl to a magical kingdom where they are met by the Sugar Plum Fairy who guides them to a throne from which they can see many different kinds of toys come to life, who dance. At the end of the night, either Drosselmeyer reappears to lead the little girl unwillingly back home, or the party just ends, and the children depart in a horse-drawn carriage, a ship, or in the case of the New York City Ballet's version, in a Santa Claus sled. The music by Tschaikovsky is glorious, the choreographies are often fun, and most mothers, grandmothers, aunts and uncles consider the various versions of *The Nutcracker* a highly suitable holiday entertainment for children, starting at about age four. Many youngsters have never seen any other ballet, but a visit to the local dance company's holiday *Nutcracker* performance is an annual family event.

Many choreographers have created dances to the Tschaikovsky score since Petipa began the first such choreography in St. Petersburg. He fell ill and the ballet was finished by an assistant. It played a few performances and somehow never became popular. In 1934, it was revived in England, and a new version, done by the Ballet Russe de Monte Carlo, was mounted in London in 1940.

But *The Nutcracker*, as a tradition, did not come alive until George Balanchine reworked it for the New York City Ballet in 1954.

Balanchine's work is a true treasure, worth seeing again and again. First of all, Balanchine casts children in the roles of children. Both Marie and her young friend are youngsters from the School of American Ballet, usually chosen to perform their first *Nutcracker* when they are nine or ten years of age. Often they continue to do these roles for several years, until they begin to look too much like teen-agers. Both children have to know how to dance and how to act. Many of the youngsters who played the roles have eventually become dancers in the company.

All the children at the party are danced by children, including a very small boy who is Marie's little brother, and who mischievously breaks the Nutcracker, which Drosselmeyer fixes.

There are certain spectacular effects in the New York City Ballet's version: a Christmas tree that grows on stage to reach up to the ceiling; a bed, in which Marie sleeps, that moves across the stage; and three large boxes of toys with figures who turn into live dancers. But what provides the real enchantment is the atmosphere that prevails throughout. The children are *children*, a little mischievous, curious, not always obedient but basically well-mannered, and above all, respectful to their elders and loving to parents and grandparents. In the family giving the party, everyone has his or her proper place. The parents obviously care for each other and for the children. The grandparents are given seats of honor and attention is paid to them.

When the children reach the land of the Sugar Plum Fairy, and the little boy tells of his victory over the Mouse King, she listens . . . respectfully. Nobody condescends to the children, ever, least of all the choreographer. Balanchine's children are treated not as cute tykes up there on the stage for older relatives to coo over. They are treated as dancers, and they perform as dancers. On the other hand, little girls whose feet are not yet fully formed are not put in toe shoes. They do their dances in soft slippers. Make-up is subtle; clothes are elegant but right for youngsters, not miniature adults.

The dances performed in the land of the Sugar Plum Fairy are small masterpieces, done by the regular company, sometimes with the addition of a small corps of young children who are given a choreography they are able to master. Not all the children who dance in the New York City Ballet's *Nutcracker* will become professional dancers. In fact, most won't. But all will remember the respect they received from the ballet master, the teachers who trained them, the adult dancers in the company . . . and most of all, Balanchine. And because they receive respect, they act respectfully. It's amazing how more than fifty young children, waiting backstage to go on for their special turn night after night, can be so well-behaved. Altogether the *Nutcracker* at the New York City Ballet is a civilized and civilizing experience for the audience and performers.

There are other *Nutcrackers* that are not nearly as beautiful or as warm and loving. For instance, there are versions in which Clara/Marie is danced by adult dancers, as are all the child-guests at the party. This rarely works. Adults pretending to be children rarely look childlike. They tend to look childish instead.

In a version choreographed by Baryshnikov for the American Ballet Theater, and adapted as an annual television event, the two "children" were danced by himself and by a wonderful, sensitive young woman, Gelsey Kirkland. It works better than most of the productions in which adults play children because Baryshnikov is so good a dancer that one forgets that he is supposed to be a little boy, and Kirkland is young enough to look like a child, and is, to top it off, a good actress. So, in some ways, that version works surprisingly well. However, the guests who are supposed to be children (including the naughty little brother who is a dancer at least five feet, ten inches tall, and another "boy" who rides a hobby horse and looks to be about thirty years of age) seem all wrong. Baryshnikov attempted to do his *Nutcracker* as a kind of allegory on growing up. The plain story, standing on its own, is much more magical.

Various companies do their own versions. Occasionally, to raise more cash, Marie/Clara and the Nutcracker Prince are played by the children of prominent members of the community. For instance, when she was a little girl, Ronald Reagan's daughter, Maureen, played Marie in a version done by the Los Angeles Ballet. These children are usually not as talented as those from the School of American Ballet and *The Nutcracker* becomes a money-raising pageant, instead of a work of art.

But fate is sometimes fair after all. *The Nutcracker* that has raised the most money is the one done annually by the New York City Ballet. This company, to date, has given 900 sold-out performances of the work since its inception in 1954. In 1980, it was seen by one hundred thousand people and raised one million four hundred thousand dollars for the company. Any event that can give so much pleasure to so many, and still make it possible for a ballet company to grow and thrive is, literally, worth its weight in gold.

When a new dancer takes over
a role in one of his ballets,
George Balanchine usually
works with him or her
to make sure that the dancing
looks exactly right.
Here Balanchine shows Baryshnikov
how to partner Patricia McBride
in a pas de deux.

Serenade was the first ballet Balanchine made for American dancers. It's still part of the regular repertory of the New York City Ballet.

The Dance Theater of Harlem
now produces some of the best
ballet dancers in the world.
Here the company is doing
a classic Fokine ballet,
Scheherazade.

Balanchine once looked at
a display of dazzling jewels and
decided to make a ballet
that would glisten and sparkle
like those stones.
Here are Suzanne Farrell and
Peter Martins in "Diamonds."
The other sections of the
ballet Jewels are "Rubies"
and "Emeralds."

Mel Tomlinson moved from the
Dance Theater of Harlem to
the New York City Ballet,
where, during his first season,
Jerome Robbins used him
as a principal dancer
in his new ballet, Concerto,
to Gershwin's Concerto in F.
New dancers usually don't get
ballets of their own during
their first season in a company.

*Two Joffrey Company principal
dancers, Denise Jackson
and Gregory Huffman.*

*The Ailey Company usually repeats
the last few minutes of its
signature piece,* Revelations.
*The applauding, shouting and
stomping audience often won't
leave the theater until it
gets an encore.*

More Alvin Ailey dancers
in one of Ailey's ethnic African
choreographies, Fanga.

Judith Jamison can fascinate
an audience just standing still.
Here she is
in Alvin Ailey's The Mooche.

*Paul Taylor dancers have to have
a special kind of energy he
calls "zunch," which is what members
of his company are showing here
in his choreography,* Polaris.

*Twyla Tharp rehearses her company.
Rehearsal clothes are among
the least glamorous ever designed.
But most dancers manage to look
fine even in such a strange
assortment of garments.*

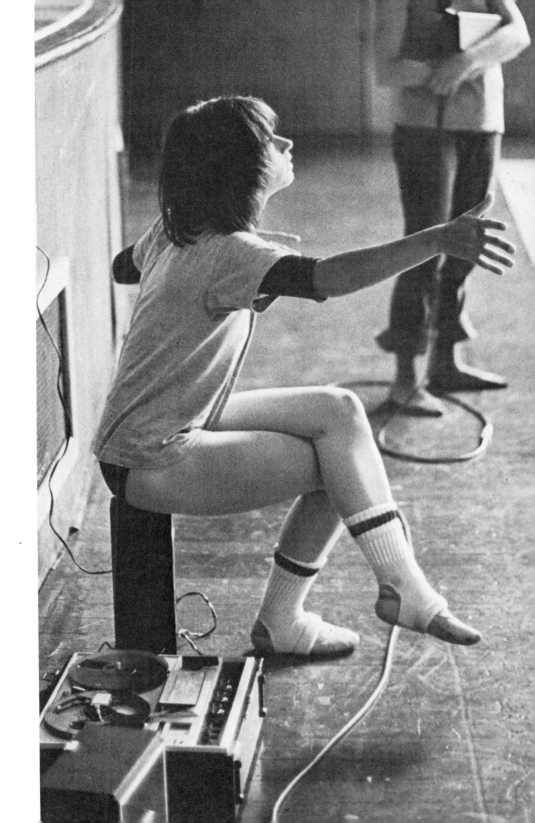

2 A Few Companies and Their Choreographers

CHAPTER VIII

The New York City Ballet and George Balanchine

"Ballet is not a democracy."
—GEORGE BALANCHINE
quoted in *Time* magazine and in several
other interviews

"It's better to tell the audience not to analyze. If you start to analyze, you'll miss the dancing . . . words are not supposed to describe music. Words cannot describe. You cannot explain a flower."
—GEORGE BALANCHINE,
talking about one of his most recent ballets
in *The World of Great Ballet* by John Gruen.

"I finally met Balanchine in the kitchen of a house leased for the London season by Kirk Askew, an excellent art dealer whom I knew from Harvard. I made a headlong onslaught; what Balanchine thought of an anonymous youth who in an exaggerated desperation promised an entire future career in half an hour, he did not say, except that he must think it over. I con-

*sole myself that, at least, or at most, it was not abso-
lutely impossible."*

—LINCOLN KIRSTEIN
in a diary entry dated July, 1933
from his book
Thirty Years: The New York City Ballet.

THERE IS no art form that has ever changed entirely and
forever in one split second except, possibly, dance. That split
second was the one in which Lincoln Edward Kirstein, a highly
educated young man and dance enthusiast from a prominent Boston family, met George Balanchine in that kitchen in London in
1933 and asked him to come to the United States to start a school
of ballet and a company of young, American-trained dancers.

The most original and brilliant part of the proposal was to
start the school before the company. The training of new dancers
had come, usually, as an afterthought, at least since the days
when the Russian aristocrats started to teach their serfs dance
steps.

The United States had never had a school for professional
ballet dancers. Ballet stars from abroad had come here and
brought enough supporting cast members with them to form at
least a nucleus of a company. If they needed more dancers, they
picked up whoever seemed most able to do rudimentary ballet
steps. The result of such efforts was, frequently, dismal. Although the imported star (almost always a ballerina) might look
magnificent, the rest of the company looked at best undertrained
and underrehearsed, and at worst just plain silly.

The School of American Ballet opened in January of 1934, on
Madison Avenue in New York City. In March of that year, work
started on the first American Balanchine ballet, to the music of
Tschaikovsky's *Serenade for Strings.* Apparently, at the time,

few realized that one of the ballet classics of all time was in the process of creation.

Kirstein remembers that *Serenade* was apparently woven by chance. Balanchine, probably with tongue in cheek, later said that he was "just trying to teach my students some little lessons and make a ballet which did not show how badly they danced." At any rate, he started by lining up seventeen girls who had appeared that day for rehearsal and class (in order of height). When one youngster slipped into the studio a few minutes after he had started to work on the choreography, he incorporated her late appearance into the form of the dance. When, a few days later only nine girls appeared, he simply did one section that featured nine instead of seventeen dancers. On another particularly bad day, only three showed up. So a section for three dancers was incorporated into the overall scheme.

When a girl tripped and fell during a rehearsal, that fall was kept in the final choreography. If all of this sounds as if the ballet turned into a kind of improvised, haphazard happening, the impression could not be more wrong. *Serenade* is one of the most beautiful and carefully planned ballets in the New York City Ballet's vast repertory of Balanchine masterpieces. It still is done every year. There are many more than seventeen girls in the company now, of course, and some of the parts are danced by soloists and principal dancers (including the girl who slips and falls). Also included in the ballet now are four male dancers.

Serenade has no story, but a very strong sense of dreamlike atmosphere, of poignant emotion and, in a sense, of the sisterhood of women dancers. The women support each other, comfort and depend on each other. Because the beauty of the choreography is based on a special quality of movement and interaction, it is difficult to describe and impossible to analyze. As Balanchine said: "You cannot explain a flower."

The theme of the Tschaikovsky score is heard before the curtain rises on rows of young women in billowing blue tulle skirts, bathed in a blue light. They are holding one arm up, with the hand turned outward, as if they were shielding their eyes from the blue light. The first movement of the ballet is the upward movement of those hands. At that point, one can usually hear a gasp from the audience. Why a simple change of hand positions can cause so much emotion is one of the secrets of Balanchine's genius.

The choreography contains a section of a waltz and of lively Russian rhythms with the dancers reflecting the music in their steps. The overall mood of the piece is one of sweet sadness and melancholy; of the ending as much as of the beginning of love.

There are regular ballet-goers who have seen *Serenade* over and over again, year after year, and who see something new and different in every performance. *Serenade* can reflect one's own mood at the time one sees it. Sometimes it seems to reflect a principal dancer's mood. It is ever changing, like a kaleidoscope, although, of course, the choreography remains the same.

It also provides a framework for understanding many of Balanchine's later romantic ballets which, although they have no specific story, give a deep and lasting impression of the feelings of men and women for each other. The Balanchine love affairs usually end sadly. His lovers meet, fall ecstatically in love, are separated by forces beyond their control (usually in the form of members of the corps de ballet who seem to get in between the lovers and keep them apart). Eventually, each of the lovers steps backwards into his or her side of the wing of the stage. But, no matter how sadly a love affair ends, one feels instinctively that Balanchine considers the ecstasy to have been worth the pain.

But most of the ballets came later. First came the school and the company. The company, which was founded and directed by Balanchine, Kirstein and a third man, Vladimir Dimitiriev (who, according to Lincoln Kirstein's book, seems to have been rather difficult and temperamental), was first called the American Ballet Company (not to be confused with the American Ballet Theater, which was founded much later). It was not initially successful. America was not yet ready for ballet on that scale. And Balanchine went off to do musicals and films. But the idea was not abandoned. In 1941, the Ballet Theater was organized, and in 1947 this name was changed to the Ballet Society, and in 1948 to the name it now bears, the New York City Ballet.

It performed first at the New York City Center, then when Lincoln Center was built, moved to the New York State Theater, which it shares with the New York City Opera. From the first the company has attempted to present first-class dance at prices all can afford. Obviously its financial problems, as a result, have always been great.

The company, under any name, may have had its problems. But because of Kirstein's devotion to the Balanchine purpose and concept, and his meticulous attention to management and finance, Balanchine has always been free to devote himself to creating new works and developing superb dancers. This he has done better than any choreographer and ballet master in history.

His background, of course, is unique, spanning almost everything that has been great in ballet for two centuries. He participated in the end of the Maryinski period, the end of Diaghilev and was also deeply involved in the great Broadway and Hollywood musicals of the mid-thirties and early forties.

Born Georgi Melitonovitch Balanchivadze (he changed his difficult, unpronounceable name when he joined Diaghilev) on January 9, 1904, in St. Petersburg, Russia, he entered the Imperial Ballet School there at the age of ten. Very early in his schooling he was chosen to dance the young boy who performs the lead in a performance of *The Nutcracker.* We presume that then, as now, the youngster picked for that important role was the one in his ballet class who showed the most stage presence and promise. At any rate, at the Maryinski he absorbed that company's tradition of classical ballet. By the time he graduated from the school in 1921, everything about his country had changed including, of course, the school and the theater. Russia was now the Soviet Union, and the Imperial Ballet School had become the Soviet State School of Ballet. Eventually St. Petersburg would change into Leningrad, and the Maryinski into the Kirov Ballet Company.

By 1923, the young dancer was already dissatisfied with what was happening in the company. He started to choreograph and organized a group of other young dancers into what was called "The Young Ballet of Petrograd." Neither his dances nor his dancers pleased the Soviet establishment. Only in 1981, when the Soviet establishment realized how dull the Russian State Ballet had become, did a magazine publish an article praising Balanchine.

In 1924, he sought and received permission to tour Germany with four other dancers, among them ballerinas Alexandra Danilova and Tamara Geva. Following their German tour, they gave a performance in Paris and there were seen by Diaghilev, who offered Balanchine and the two women positions in his company. Balanchine never went back to Russia to live, although eventually, he toured that country with dancers from the New York City Ballet.

During his four years with Diaghilev he choreographed several important ballets, including *The Prodigal Son*, which is still in the repertory of many leading ballet companies. In 1980, Baryshnikov danced it with the New York City Ballet, and in 1981, with the American Ballet Theater

Three years after Diaghilev's death, that company was disbanded and Balanchine joined the new Ballet Russe de Monte Carlo. He became its principal choreographer, and it was in this group that Kirstein first saw him, both as a dancer and as a choreographer. The invitation to come to the United States followed.

The company that eventually emerged, the New York City Ballet, was not appreciated immediately. Balanchine's approach to ballet, the dances that did not tell stories but created movement with music and an often indefinable mood or atmosphere, were a drastic change from any dances the public, especially the American public, had seen. He not only changed the content of dance, but the way the dancers looked. Often they wore no recognizable costumes: dancers appeared in what seemed to be rehearsal clothes, black or white tunics and tights on the women, black tights and white tee shirts on the men. There was little scenery. Audiences may have suspected that the absence of elaborate stage design and costumes might have been due to lack of money. Perhaps in part, this was true. But some of Balanchine's best ballets look best in the simplest possible settings and costumes. The movement of the dancers' bodies, the lines and patterns created by the steps, are what one really comes to see. Costumes and scenery are not only unnecessary; they probably would get in the way.

It is difficult to describe the Balanchine style, just as it is impossible to describe one of his nonstory ballets.

Balanchine does not like to be interviewed. When he talks to reporters and dance reviewers, one often gets the feeling that he uses words to hide meanings, rather than to express them. Every word is closely thought out, but it is often the listener who has to look for the meaning behind the words to try to discover what, exactly, it is that Balanchine is saying.

In an interview that appeared in the magazine, *Saturday Review*, in August of 1981, he answered reporter Kitty Cunningham's question about how he created ballet "from the ground up" like this: "People always ask me to explain how I make a ballet. I answer that I create out of necessity. We have to do

something for the people who come to see our company. We try
to make different things: a short piece, a long piece, a piece with
lots of people, a work that uses light music, or French or German
music. So, it's necessity, never inspiration. What is inspiration?
It doesn't exist. It isn't tangible. It's like a soul, it's there, but it
is not. Something that exists—like necessity—is much more important."

When asked if he planned steps for a new dance "at home,"
he said: "No. Does a writer think of words? Steps are like words;
they only mean something in the studio when you come in and
start the steps, like putting words together to make a piece of
writing. I have to do the steps for the ballets, I cannot sit back
and talk about it. It's better to go to sleep and to rest at home,
rather than think, because dancers are moving people and we
need rest too."

The most basic element in all of Balanchine's work is the
music. Whether he is composing to a Mozart divertimento, a
Tschaikovsky concerto, a group of Vienna waltzes, Gershwin
songs or Sousa marches, the skeleton under the choreography is
always the music. He does not just listen to it; he reads scores.
"The only way to know the music is to read the scores," he says.
"When you listen by ear, you don't understand. You must look
at the score . . . You see, your ears are not perfect, your eyes are
not perfect. Each person hears differently and sees differently."

When Balanchine founded the company that would eventually become the New York City Ballet, he was sure of one
important detail: he did not wish to build his company around
star dancers. A no-star company is what he had in mind, and
what, at least on paper, he still has.

His first ballet was made for a group of young students, and
he fitted his choreographies to their capacities. He still does that.
The capabilities of his dancers seem to influence his work almost
as much as the music. He has trained a group of extraordinary
dancers who can perform technical feats that are, generally, beyond those who have not received their training at the School of
American Ballet. The women in the company are unlike any
other group of women dancers anywhere in the world, and with
one exception, they are all American and have received most of
their training in his school. Yet each dancer is an individual, with
individual style and ability, and he uses those special talents by
creating special roles for special people.

The no-star policy works in the company's publicity. The casts are, for instance, not announced in newspapers before performances. You come to see a ballet or a series of ballets, not a special dancer or group of dancers. Many of the company's policies, as well as the fact that casts are not advertised, are tailored to the no-star concept. Corps members are paid better than their colleagues in other companies. There are no astronomically high salaries for the principal dancers. A situation in which a corps member makes less than ten thousand dollars per year and a star principal more than one hundred fifty thousand dollars (one that until recently was true for The American Ballet Theater), would simply be impossible at the City Ballet.

But the dancers for whom ballets were originally made or who have been groomed especially for a role by Balanchine himself have become stars in the minds of the ballet-going public. They will go to see a ballet like *Chaconne* no matter who is dancing, but most would much prefer to see Peter Martins and Suzanne Farrell, for whom the choreography was made, as the principal dancers. They really want to see Patricia McBride, for whom *Coppelia* was choreographed, in that role even though it has been very competently danced by a younger member of the company, Stephanie Saland. In 1980 and 1981, there was always a special demand for tickets when it became known that a sensational teen-ager, Darci Kistler, was going to be in the cast of anything.

But dancers have come, and dancers have gone, at the New York City Ballet. Usually, principals remain for as long as they are able to dance . . . only rarely does anyone leave, even when other companies offer much higher salaries and star treatment. As one dancer is no longer able to perform a role, another usually steps in and makes it his or her own. The company has a kind of continuity that few other dance groups in the world can maintain. But that continuity depends at least partly on the graying, but still young-looking, Balanchine, who is listed on the program simply as one of the four ballet masters (although his name heads the list). The general director, incidentally, is still Lincoln Kirstein.

What will happen to the company when Balanchine must retire (he is past his middle seventies and had open heart surgery several years ago), no one really knows. He is, of course, the real star of that company, and his role cannot be filled like that of a principal dancer. Certainly the dancers themselves know this. Even though Mr. B., as they all call him, rules not only their professional lives, but also their personal lives, not one of them can imagine what life would be like without him.

It is Balanchine whom the dancers watch as they come off-stage after a new role or an especially demanding performance. No amount of audience applause or critical acclaim matters to them as much as a word of approval from him. If he ignores one of them for a while, that person can become severely depressed. If he praises someone, that person's day or even week is made. Balanchine decides who dances what, who is promoted, who is told that someone else will be dancing a favorite role from now on. They love him and they fear him. But above all, they respect him because they know that there never was anyone like him before in the history of dance, nor is there likely to be anyone quite like him again.

Once, two elderly dance critics were talking about the fate of ballet in this century. One was bemoaning the loss of the Maryinski Theater. "Where or when will we see anything like that again?" he plaintively asked his friend. "Right here and now, at the New York State Theater in Lincoln Center," the friend answered. "The body of the Maryinski might still be at the Kirov in Leningrad . . . but the spirit is in the New York City Ballet. And you can add to that the spirit of Diaghilev and the best of Broadway and Hollywood . . . dancing has never been better anywhere at any time."

CHAPTER IX

More
New York City Ballet:
Jerome Robbins
and Others

*Robbins and Balanchine work as a duet in tandem.
Both are secure in endowment and practice to compete
where there is no need for competition. They are separated by nearly twenty years, yet their joint respect
for music as a floor for dancing can forge no finer
bond.*

—LINCOLN KIRSTEIN
in *Thirty Years: The New York City Ballet*

J EROME ROBBINS'S name appears right under that of Balanchine as ballet master on the New York City Ballet program.
But, as Kirstein indicates, there probably is no competition be-

tween the two men. Their artistic roots are as different as their choreographic styles.

Where Balanchine's earliest beginnings were in Russia and France, in Petipa and the Diaghilev Company, Robbins is pure American. Born in New York City, his experience and training as a dancer, director and choreographer had its principal beginnings, not in classical ballet, but on the Broadway stage and in films.

There are echoes of Broadway in many of his finest ballet choreographies, often combined with whiffs of an ethnic Jewish nostalgia. One has the feeling that his parents, or at least his grandparents, often must have discussed life in a *stetl*, a small Jewish village in Eastern Europe. This particular element of his talent is most evident in *Fiddler on the Roof*, which he directed. It tells the story of a Jewish family living in one of those villages in Tzarist Russia. The dances in that Broadway hit show, which eventually became a highly successful movie, are clearly influenced by the Jewish folk dances Robbins probably saw as a youngster, or at least heard described. And some of this kind of dancing shows up in some of his ballets, most notably in a choreography he made for the New York City Ballet called *Dybbuk Variations.* Upon seeing it danced, one is reminded of the dances often done at weddings and other celebrations by Hassidic Jews in Jerusalem, Israel or Brooklyn, New York.

His Broadway style is evident in *Fancy Free*, his finest ballet, the story of three sailors on leave, which was expanded into a highly successful Broadway musical, *On the Town*. That show, too, eventually became a film with dancer Gene Kelly in the cast, but did not reproduce the great choreography of its Broadway predecessor.

Robbins, like all choreographers was, of course, first a dancer. In an interview, he answered, almost indignantly, a question about whether it was really necessary to be a dancer before starting to make dances for others. "Of course, you have to dance," he said. "How else would you know what steps are possible, how the body moves?" Unlike Balanchine, who as a dancer performed only in ballet, Robbins not only studied but performed in a variety of dance forms: Spanish, modern, tap, jazz. All of these influences can be seen in his ballets, although with the exception of *Fancy Free* and one children's ballet, *Mother Goose* (which tells several fairy tales), none is specifically a story ballet.

Actually, Robbins's first ballets, *Fancy Free* and *Interplay* (a choreography that features several young dancers who seem to be teen-agers on a New York City street), were made for the American Ballet Theater. But much of his best work has been done for the New York City Ballet, which he joined twice—from 1949 to 1963, and then again from 1969 to the present.

Besides *Fancy Free* and *Interplay*, which are now in the regular repertory of both the New York City Ballet and the American Ballet Theater, several of the early Robbins works are still performed during most seasons. Among them is the funniest of all existing ballets, *The Concert or the Perils of Everybody*. There are other ballets that are meant to make the audience laugh, but in all of them it is the story, not the dancing, that provides the amusement.

Robbins is the only choreographer to date who has been able to use classic ballet steps and positions in combinations that, in and of themselves, are wildly funny. He has created characters who are comic and still dance in strictly classic ballet style. With the exception of the pianist (always one of the regular New York City Ballet solo pianists), who is on stage playing on a concert grand the Chopin pieces that provide the music, all comic effects are achieved through dancing with a minimal amount of mime.

These characters are amazingly apt caricatures of concert-goers who spend an evening listening to music, not necessarily because they enjoy it, but because they want to show others how cultured and civilized they are. There is a bookish gentleman who seemingly would like to convey the idea that he is concentrating on what he is hearing. He is followed into the "concert hall" by two chattering young women who clearly wish they were spending the evening playing bridge, rather than having to listen to Chopin. Then there is a girl who obviously is more interested in impressing the pianist with her ardor and admiration than in listening to what he is playing. What's more, she is equally concerned with attracting the attention of every other male in the audience.

Then in walks a cigar-chewing gentleman who reminds one of the way Archie Bunker might look if he were forced to attend a piano recital instead of a football game. He is followed by his nagging, hen-pecking wife, the kind of culture vulture who, one just knows, often drags her poor reluctant husband to concerts and other similar mind-improving occasions. The last two people to enter are a shy boy and a very aggressive, angry young woman. Everybody is in the wrong seat. After a frantic usher has straightened out the seating arrangements, the concert can proceed.

At this point, everyone plays out a favorite fantasy. The henpecked husband stabs his wife (who even in his daydream flatly refuses to die), the shy boy drags off the lady enamored of the pianist. The lady finds just the perfect hat at a boutique, only to discover that four other woman are wearing the same headgear. And so it goes.

There is even a fantasy for some dancers who are only incidental members of the audience of this disastrous concert. They put on what is called *The Mistake Waltz*. Everybody gets all their steps wrong, points their feet in the wrong direction, lets arms droop and, in short, manages to make every dance mistake that would be immediately and sternly corrected in class. Only here they are allowed to make all those errors on stage.

At the end of the piece, the pianist, who decides he has suffered enough, stops playing, gets a butterfly net, and as the curtain goes down is seen chasing all those weird characters, who by now have grown wings, around the stage.

The ballet is the Keystone Cops, Jerry Lewis and Company, and *Saturday Night Live* all rolled into one, yet it is in strictly classical ballet style and to some of Chopin's best-known piano music. It is a true comic masterpiece.

Another Robbins' choreography, done to the Debussy score of *Afternoon of a Faun*, tells a completely different story from the original *Faun* choreographed by Nijinsky. Robbins's inspiration for this ballet came not from the Greek friezes that had inspired Nijinsky, but from the sight of a young male dancer in an empty rehearsal studio working out at the barre while watching himself in one of the full-length mirrors that line the walls of all dance practice halls.

The set for the ballet is just such a hall, made up of white sheets representing mirrors and lined with a barre on the three sides of the stage that do not face the audience. The side toward the audience is supposed to be another mirror in which the two young dancers, who make up the whole cast of the ballet, observe themselves as they go through their practice routines. Looking at the set in another way, the eyes of the audience are also the reflections of the images the dancers see of themselves and each other.

The story line of the ballet is a very simple one. As the curtain rises, a young male dancer is seen lying on his back on the floor, probably asleep. He stirs briefly, stretches, arches his back and sits up. He never takes his eyes from the imaginary mirror, the audience. He stands, somersaults, lies down on his stomach, and goes back to sleep.

A young woman dancer in practice clothes, her hair loose to the waist, enters. She doesn't notice the man. Her eyes, as she does her warm-up routine, are entirely on herself, her image in the mirror. The man wakes up, notices her and stands behind her, doing some special exercises with her. He lifts her up. Both their eyes are still firmly fixed on the mirror. They go through what looks like a preliminary rehearsal for a pas de deux, never for a second looking at each other, only at their now joined images in the mirror. Eventually, the man, kneeling next to the ballerina, lightly kisses her on the cheek. For a split second she looks at him and, observing that he is still absorbed in his own image, she turns away, stands and backs out of the practice room. The curtain falls.

This short ballet tells more about a dancer's self-image, the complete absorption in body movement and attitude that dancing demands, than volumes of books about the lives and attitudes of the young men and women who dance professionally.

Dancers, of course, live their lives surrounded by mirrors. They have learned to look at their bodies as if they were objects outside of themselves, objects that they must criticize as if they did not even belong to them. This attitude has nothing to do with vanity. Indeed, it often leads to the opposite. Since no movement ever reaches the kind of perfection that every dancer yearns for, dancers tend to be supercritical of their bodies. Robbins knows that well. After all, he was a dancer himself, and in a way, still is. What seems so amazing about this particular choreography is how, in a matter of minutes, he can show something about dancers that psychologists would take volumes to explore.

After his early years with the New York City Ballet, Robbins briefly formed his own company: Ballet USA. But mainly his work was concentrated on Broadway musicals: *The King and I*; *Peter Pan* (in which Mary Martin danced through the air suspended on a thin wire); *West Side Story*; and *Gypsy*. In *West Side Story*, he used dance in a way that had not been used since Agnes de Mille's *Oklahoma*, as an absolutely essential, integral part of the story. Indeed, *West Side Story* is almost, but not quite, a pure dance musical. Certainly all of the conflicts that rend the principal characters and their communities apart are shown in terms of dance. The two street gangs that make up the opposing forces dance their battles against each other and society as a whole.

This musical was revived in New York in 1980. Its sociological message seemed dated, even simplistic. But the dancing, particularly that depicting the anger and frustration of the youngsters in the two opposing gangs, was as wonderful and as timely as ever. Probably because of the Robbins' choreography, *West Side Story* is still a moving and artistically valid experience.

In *Fiddler On The Roof*, which Robbins directed, nondancers are used to perform the folk dances of the Russian stetl. Even when no one on stage is actually dancing, the expert hand of the choreographer is clearly visible in the production. Robbins moves a group of people around on a stage in ways that only a choreographer would do.

Since his return to the New York City Ballet, a steady flow of new choreographies by Robbins have been produced. Usually there are two or three per season. Among the ballets that are great audience and critics' favorites, *Dances at a Gathering*, a serious choreography also to Chopin's piano music, stands out. The ballet is performed by many other companies, even some in Europe, and is one of the dances Robbins brought to China with him when he visited that country at the government's invitation in the summer of 1981, taking a number of New York City Ballet dancers with him.

Although the majority of programs at the New York City Ballet are still formed principally of Balanchine and Robbins works, lately principal dancer Peter Martins seems to have joined the ranks of regular choreographers. Martins's main task in the company is still dancing, but he has been asked to do two or three special choreographies every season for the past three years, and much of what he has done is original and beautiful. Martins is, of course, much younger than either of the two principal choreographers. Also, he has always worshipped Balanchine and his work. For him, getting free enough of the Balanchine influence to become a completely original choreographer must be a difficult task. Much of his latest work, which ranges from a short Stravinsky tango for ice skater John Curry, to three movements of the First Tschaikovsky Symphony for the 1981 Tschaikovsky

Festival, shows that he is beginning to use his own dance vocabulary and that, eventually, he will almost certainly be able to step out of his mentor's shadow to do exciting work on his own. The company also performs regularly a few ballets by dancer Jacques d'Amboise and Ballet Master John Taras.

For the continuity of a dance company as great as the New York City Ballet, it is important to have young, gifted choreographers come up from the ranks, just as new young dancers join the older, experienced ones year after year.

CHAPTER X

The American Ballet Theater: The Classics, The European Choreographers, Agnes de Mille and More Robbins

There is a bond between the American Ballet Theater and former members. Even those of us who have left it occasionally to pursue other challenges have never felt completely separated from it. . . . The lure of the company is as strong as ever. Its primary attraction for all of us has been the range of its repertory and yet, for each of us, it has its own unique appeal.

—NORA KAYE, one of America's first great ballerinas, producer of the motion picture *The Turning Point* (which featured the American Ballet Theater), and associate director of that company.

THE AMERICAN BALLET THEATER (ABT) and the New York City Ballet (NYCB) sprang from the same root. The American Ballet was founded, as was recorded in a previous chapter, by Lincoln Kirstein and George Balanchine. After a first season of two weeks in 1935, the company was suspended and Kirstein formed a company made up of a few Balanchine students. He called it The Ballet Caravan; it disbanded in 1941.

Meanwhile, another ballet company, the Mordkin Ballet, was performing in the United States, headed by Russian choreographer Michel Fokine. Out of the remnants of the Ballet Caravan and the Mordkin Ballet, the Ballet Theater was formed. This company was, to use a technical term, "eclectic." That meant that it would perform the traditional story ballets, some new story ballets by American and European choreographers, and some nonstory ballets by some still unknown Americans.

Later this group broke up and one splinter group, The Ballet Society, took both Kirstein and Balanchine, who had been a part of it, so what was left as The Ballet Theater had to look for new leadership. They were lucky to find exactly what was needed: Lucia Chase, an exceedingly wealthy woman, devoted to ballet, who had danced herself but had not succeeded as an artist. She was, however, a genius at management and fund-raising. "The achievements of the American Ballet Theater, as well as its survival, are due to the passion, the unremitting concern and generosity of one patron, Lucia Chase, whose gift in terms of money equals, or possibly surpasses, that of any single patron of any cultural institution in the United States. In terms of energy and dedication she is unmatched," writes Agnes de Mille in her book *America Dances.* "For over forty years she has given all her time, all day and night, summer and winter, as well as her faculties, all her will, all her steady patience, endurance and sanity. What she has built is the longest-lasting ballet theater in the nation, and one of high excellence. . . ."

Lucia Chase and scene designer Oliver Smith, served as co-directors of the company from its inception until 1980, when Mikhail Baryshnikov was appointed to fill the post of artistic director. No one was appointed to succeed Oliver Smith. Apparently, the company's board of directors felt that only one person was needed to head the group.

Although both ABT and NYCB sprang from the same roots, the only similarities left between the two companies are that they are both ballet companies and are headquartered at Lincoln Center.

The differences are vast. The philosophy behind the two companies is different, the repertory is different, the attitude towards the dancers is different, and even the audience is different.

Each company has its devoted fans. For a balletomane devoted to the Balanchine company to argue the merits of his favorite with a balletomane devoted to ABT would not only be useless, it might even end in a fight. At a dinner party of regular ballet-goers, one would no more start a discussion about the relative merits of the two companies than one would argue politics or religion.

The American Ballet Theater does not now and never has had a resident choreographer; while the New York City Ballet has had at least two: Balanchine and Robbins, and possibly now a third: Martins. ABT specializes in evening-long classic ballets: *Swan Lake, Giselle, Don Quixote, Sleeping Beauty,* the Petipa masterpieces of the Russian Imperial Ballet. NYCB does none of these; the company does a version of *Swan Lake,* made by Balanchine, which uses some of the Tschaikovsky music, almost none of the original choreography, and takes about fifteen minutes. Actually it is not the Petipa *Swan Lake* at all, but a sort of commentary Balanchine makes on the original choreography.

ABT, perhaps twice a week, does a program they call "a mixed bill," featuring several short ballets. Many are also story ballets: Agnes de Mille's *Rodeo,* for instance, or even Jerome Robbins' *Fancy Free.* But what the company is known for and what its patrons expect are the classic, all-evening nineteenth century princes and princesses.

While NYCB rigorously tries to enforce its no-star policy (Even Baryshnikov was treated, as much as possible, like every other dancer when he was a member of that company), ABT revels in its stars, and often pays them salaries in six figures. The patrons who come to see ABT performances come to see particular performers more than they do particular ballets. Baryshnikov, now back with ABT as artistic director as well as a dancer, can sell out the house, no matter what he does. His fans will stand in line for hours to buy a ticket to see him in *Swan Lake* or *Sleeping Beauty* even though the principal male character in these particular ballets has very little to do but partner the ballerina.

Who is dancing what is usually announced in advertisements in *The New York Times* and other publications about three weeks before a performance. And who is dancing makes all the difference. There can be three *Swan Lakes* in a row, one with Baryshnikov and the other two without him, and the Baryshnikov performance will be sold out with scalpers lurking in the corners to sell tickets at wildly inflated prices, while the two non-Baryshnikov performances may be playing to a lot of empty seats.

In a way this is not really the fault of either the company or the audience. It has just happened that way over the years. Indeed, ABT is continuing a tradition that was almost universal for American ballet-goers when important stars were imported from abroad. Today, the system does not work very well.

In the first place, America is probably now training the best dancers in the world. There is almost no one we can import who can dance better than at least twelve American dancers, with one or two outstanding exceptions: Baryshnikov and Natalia Makarova. ABT found this out only a few years ago. When the Bolshoi star Aleksandr Godunov defected from his company, which was dancing in New York, to almost hysterical publicity from the media, ABT immediately signed him up. Anyone who had seen him dance with the Bolshoi during that company's New York performances knew he was an adequate dancer—better than most of the men in the Russian company—but not really better than at least three American-trained dancers already working at ABT.

He received a six-figure salary. The corps members, who were all making less than ten thousand dollars per year revolted. It wasn't that they didn't like Godunov, a good looking, pleasant young man. They simply felt that the star system had gone too far . . . and it had.

ABT has its stars. Except for Baryshnikov and Natalia Makarova, they are mostly American: Cynthia Gregory, Marianna Tcherkassky, Fernando Bujones, and until 1981, Gelsey Kirkland, who will, everyone hopes, return again in the years to come. On the world scene, there are a few dancers who can rival our own native product. Looking around at other companies, there just don't seem to be any more Baryshnikovs or Makarovas around for ABT to acquire. It therefore becomes doubly important for the company to develop its own top dancers, and for that purpose, a no-star policy seems to be much more effective than the traditional policy of ABT.

The new artistic director, Baryshnikov, has spent enough time at the Kirov, which, unlike the Bolshoi, emphases repertory and overall quality of dancing, and with NYCB, which would not dream of paying any dancer a six-figure salary (nor keeping its corps on starvation wages), so that he has already made some changes.

ABT, of course, will continue to dance the classics. Baryshnikov, like Balanchine, looks back at the Maryinski days (unlike Balanchine, he never experienced them personally) with love and respect. Indeed, he is trying to redesign some of the ABT classics to conform more closely to the original Petipa choreographies. But he also likes to encourage new, young choreographers and may be expected to commission works from some *American* artists, including several who have not made ballets previously, but have worked in a variety of other dance disciplines.

Also, like Balanchine, he believes in hiring dancers who can advance through the corps to become, eventually, principals. In order to do this, he knows that he will have to encourage them to dance principal roles while they are still corps members. In his first year as artistic director, he did exactly that. He himself danced Balanchine's *The Prodigal Son* (a choreography new to the company, incidentally), but he alternated with another gifted young dancer who at the time was still a corps member.

The company has had its own school for decades. But the school accepted nonprofessionals as well as those who wished to make dancing their life's work. The company hired very few of that school's graduates. Dancers had a better chance of making it into the ABT corps from the School of American Ballet, directed by Balanchine, or even from one of the excellent schools in Washington, D.C. or Salt Lake City, Utah, than from the company's own school. The company also hired many graduates from German, French and Dutch schools.

Now, the management expects to train its own dancers as NYCB has done from the beginning. In 1981, the new ABT School opened with about thirty students, a drastic reduction from its earlier numbers. But each of these students had been carefully auditioned, many by the artistic director himself. All had already spent many years in other good ballet schools, and all expect to work professionally as dancers. Amateurs were out . . . no matter how much tuition they were willing and able to pay.

It is difficult to know at this time how the repertory of the company will change, but there certainly is a tradition from the past that is well worth maintaining. For instance, some outstanding American ballets are performed primarily by this company. Among them are two by Agnes de Mille: *Rodeo* with a lively, syncopated score by American composer Aaron Copland, and *Fall River Legend* with music by another American composer, Morton Gould.

Both also tell uniquely American stories, although *Rodeo* may seem old-fashioned to many of today's young women. It concerns a cowgirl who wants to be a cowboy. She refuses to dress up like all the other young women on the ranch. She tries to ride broncos and rope cows, like the men. She struts and boasts of her skills, but is basically forlorn and insecure because none of the men who are courting the "feminine girls" will pay the slightest bit of attention to her. Eventually she sees the error of her ways, dresses in what is considered at the ranch an appropriately girlish manner and catches the man she has always wanted. The message of the ballet, "if you are a girl who wants to attract a man you'd better forget about your individuality and behave and look like all the other girls," seems inappropriate these days. After all, almost all young women wear blue jeans and somehow manage not to repel all potential suitors, but the dancing in the piece is lively, amusing and often moving. It is a choreography well worth keeping.

Fall River Legend is a completely different ballet. The story is about Lizzie Borden, a young, frustrated, repressed and ill-treated woman who is suspected of having murdered her father and her particularly cruel and obnoxious stepmother. It's an event that actually happened. In real life, Lizzie was put on trial and eventually acquitted, although the murder was never solved. In the ballet no doubt is left: Lizzie, driven into a frenzy by her parents' cruelty, does indeed murder them with an axe. This may sound like a story more suitable for the front page of the *National Enquirer* than for a ballet, but it works exceedingly well. It is another one of the de Mille ballets that should be preserved; and the only way to preserve a ballet is to keep dancing it.

Since its beginnings in 1940, ABT has performed that service for many European as well as American choreographies. Although Robbins' *Fancy Free* and *Interplay* are also danced by NYCB, his *Les Noces* is not. A true masterpiece about a Middle European arranged wedding, done to the music of Stravinsky, it has remained in the repertory of ABT. This ballet requires a choir as well as a large orchestra, and regional ballet companies just cannot afford to perform it. So it is one of the choreographies that remain with us because ABT does it.

Then there are ballets by British choreographers that other American companies simply don't do, or do only rarely. Among them is *Jardin aux Lilas* or *The Lilac Garden,* an exceedingly romantic story ballet by English choreographer Anthony Tudor. The ballet, to the music by French composer Ernest Chausson, has an old-fashioned story about a young girl forced into a loveless marriage with a middle-aged man when she truly loves a young officer. Again, the content is old-fashioned, but the choreography is lovely and well worth preserving.

ABT also does several exciting and beautiful ballets by another British choreographer, Sir Frederick Ashton, which would probably not be seen in this country if the ABT did not perform them regularly.

Many of the ballets that this company performs require expensive scenery and costumes, which no other company can afford. Usually the stage design and lighting are superb, and because pieces remain in the repertory for years, the money spent on fine garments and good scenery can be amortized over many seasons, another reason why it is important to keep ABT in good artistic and financial shape.

The company, as mentioned before, has a very loyal following, and, from the point of view of financial security, much of this following is affluent enough to afford the very expensive tickets (fifty dollars in the orchestra), and to contribute to the annual fund drives as well as attending the various galas, which often require donations of $500 or more for one seat. At ABT one sees many more mink coats and diamond earrings in the audience (at least in the orchestra, boxes and grand tier) than one does blue jeans or turtleneck sweaters.

The list of patrons includes some of America's top industrial and social leaders, among them Jackie Kennedy Onassis. Since ABT needs all the money the company can raise to remain alive and well, this is probably a healthy development. Certainly the younger, less affluent NYCB audience and patrons would have a very hard time keeping a company that needs a budget like ABT going . . . and, even for those who belong to the NYCB faction, the idea that ABT would have to shrink in size and scope, or fail altogether for lack of funds, is unthinkable.

CHAPTER XI

The Joffrey and The Alvin Ailey Dance Theater

The Joffrey Company's guiding intelligence has been the director's taste. The record is more than good. The company has had its moments of greatness. Unique in its exuberance of style, a repository of masterpieces rescued from oblivion, and for many, an introduction to ballet, the Joffrey has played a vital role in the development of dance in the United States.

—Dance critic ANNA KISSELGOFF
in *The New York Times*

His size, combined with the expression of concern that shapes his mouth and his eyes, always makes me think of Smokey Bear, warning us to be careful. His face shows a perpetual solicitude for all those talented people who can be wasted for a lifetime by one moment of inattention. Alvin is a guardian, dedicated to protecting the heritage of the past, and the seeds of the future. His father was a farmer, and he knows that neither crops nor people grow without being tended.

—JOSEPH H. MAZO writing about Ailey
in *The Alvin Ailey American Dance Theater.*

THE JOFFREY is a ballet group that often looks like a modern dance company. The Alvin Ailey group is a modern dance company that often looks like a cross between a Broadway show and ballet. Both make their headquarters in New York City and, during their annual New York season, dance at the City Center. However, they spend much of their time touring the United States and Europe, and are regarded as national, rather than regional New York companies.

The beginnings of the Joffrey Company, about twenty-five years ago, sounds a little like one of those early Judy Garland-Mickey Rooney movies in which everybody gets together in somebody's barn to put on a show. "Hey kids, let's all pitch in, make the scenery out of cardboard and the costumes out of flour sacks. Perhaps Mom would lend us some old sheets for curtains . . . and we'll invite the whole town for the opening." Robert Joffrey, who says that he cannot remember ever having wanted to do anything but run a ballet company, loaded himself and five friends into a borrowed station wagon with some recorded music, minimal costumes, scenery that was indeed made of cardboard, and started touring the country, inviting everybody to the opening.

The company was built by touring, playing in makeshift theaters and college auditoriums in a series of one-night stands. The group began with no financial backing, and the dancers performed often without getting paid more than room and board in whatever community they happened to find an audience or a theater owner willing to give them a stage on which to dance.

Eventually, the station wagon was replaced by a bus. The company first got one pianist and then two, and finally a small chamber orchestra. They toured for almost ten years before they ever danced in Manhattan. (They had one performance in the Brooklyn Academy of Music somewhere along the way.)

Today there are forty dancers in the Joffrey, plus a small group of apprentices, generally called "Joffrey II," who have studied ballet but are not yet quite ready to join the main troupe. Among the Joffrey II dancers is a son of the President of the United States. Ronald Reagan Jr. left Yale University, where he had been a sophomore, took some ballet lessons and auditioned for Joffrey II. He was accepted. In January of 1982, he was still with Joffrey II and had appeared with the main company only as a member of a few crowd scenes, when everybody, including students, apprentices and Joffrey II members are used to fill up the stage.

The Reagans, at first, seemed to feel slightly embarassed about having a son who was a ballet dancer. During the Presidential campaign, they volunteered no information about Ron Jr. until a reporter asked about him. Then President Reagan found it necessary to tell the press that, although he was a dancer, "Ron is a *real* man." What this did, of course, was to reemphasize the outmoded idea that male dancers are, for some obscure reason, effeminate. Since then the Reagans have attended a few performances in which their son participated, and Nancy Reagan, in her capacity as First Lady, headed a fund drive gala for the Joffrey in 1981.

The Joffrey has two resident choreographers with very different dance styles. Robert Joffrey himself made a great many dances for the company in the early years, but has cut down on choreography in recent times to concentrate on managing the group and raising enough money to keep it going. Much of the company's repertory is now made up of dances by the associate artistic director, Gerald Arpino. Both Joffrey's and Arpino's choreographies tend to be youth-oriented. They use a lot of hard rock, for instance, and Joffrey's best known ballet, *Astarte,* is designed to be a multimedia experience with images superimposed on other images, flashing lights, pictures projected from film slides, and a score by the Crome Syrcus rock band. It made the cover of *Time* when it opened in 1967, and as one critic put it: "Evidently the time was ripe for *Astarte:* audiences went in droves to this tuned-in, turned out, dropped out, flipped out spectacle."

Arpino too has been much influenced by the youth culture. His ballet *Trinity* is full of flower-children and their symbolism. It too is scored with hard rock music, occasionally varied with religious chants. Audiences love it; critics often don't. Arpino also uses Baroque and eighteenth-century classical themes for what are usually termed modern ballet choreographies. For instance, in *Viva Vivaldi* he uses that early composer to make a ballet that looks a little like a Mexican folk dance. In *Light Rain,* he uses parts of a Mozart piano concerto to score a pas de deux for a couple who seem to spend a great deal of time rolling around on the floor together.

Arpino has made dances for Broadway musicals as well as for ballet, and his style tends to be a mixture of what is highly popular with what might be considered a version of classical dance.

These days, Joffrey's choreographies have become more classical. One of his recent ballets, *Postcards,* to the music of French impressionist composer Erik Satie, looks like something a conservative choreographer like Sir Frederick Ashton might have done: men and women dressed in fashions of the turn-of-the-century, doing a series of restrained but beautifully developed dances, separately and in groups.

However, the Joffrey's principal contribution to dance is that company has, as part of its repertory, *preserved* some wonderful dances that might have been lost. Rudolf Nureyev used the entire company in his *Tribute to Diaghilev* series, which he performed at a New York Theater and which was later filmed for public television as *Tribute to Nijinsky.* It was probably Nureyev himself who attempted to reconstruct some of the work done by the Diaghilev Company, but the Joffrey dancers caught the style beautifully, and now that the work is on film, other dancers will be able to look at these dances and reproduce them.

Joffrey also has rescued from oblivion a truly magnificent antiwar ballet by a German choreographer, Kurt Jooss, who organized a dance group in Essen, Germany, in 1932, just before Hitler took over the government and closed down the group. The ballet, *The Green Table,* shows what the stupidity of diplomats can do to the lives of all people involved in war. Death, in the end, overtakes generals and war profiteers along with everyone else. This choreography might be considered prophetic in view of what happened to Germany a few years later. The Joffrey dancers do it brilliantly; and seeing it, one wishes it could be taken to the General Assembly of the United Nations and be performed there with all the delegates required to attend.

THE AILEY COMPANY is an entirely different kind of dance group. Although Ailey himself started it as an integrated group, it consists mainly of black dancers who have had superb training in a variety of dance disciplines, including ballet, modern dance, jazz and tap. Many of the choreographies done by the company are by Ailey himself. He has, however, commissioned others to make dances for the group in recent years. Many of the dances are on black folk themes, some resemble Broadway show pieces, and still others cannot be characterized in any specific way except that they look like some of the best choreography done for modern dance in America today.

The signature piece of the company is *Revelations*, done to black American spirituals. The performance features a choir as well as an orchestra. One critic called it, "A brilliant evocation of the black experience, tracing its evolution from the oppression of slavery through exultation in freedom and a final triumph of the spirit." If all of this sounds uplifting, but somewhat dull, the impression could not be less correct. Of all American dances, *Revelations* probably has more unadulterated joy and fun in it than anything else made in the last fifty years. It invariably brings the audience to its feet and, of all the dance companies in the world, the Ailey group may be the only one that ever does an encore. *Revelations* is always last on the program, and the audience just refuses to leave. Usually, the dancers manage to do the rousing finale, to the spiritual "Rock My Soul in the Bosom of Abraham," over again.

There are moments in this dance that are truly unforgettable: a tall, beautiful woman (formerly Ailey's top dancer, Judith Jamison, but now one of the other principals) dancing to "Take Me to the Water" with an enormous white umbrella, and later, three men, leaping and turning to "Sinner Man" in high style. Never has sin looked like so much fun.

Ailey has commissioned a number of black musicians and choreographers to create special dances for his company. Many have gone on to work for other dance groups, but he gave them their first chance. In more recent seasons, he has also commissioned white and Oriental choreographers. In the 1981 season, a marvelous, very balletic choreography by Chinese-American choreographer Choo San Goh was introduced.

The Ailey Company loses regularly some of its best dancers to Broadway and other dance groups. Judith Jamison, for instance, has been starring in the hit Broadway show *Sophisticated Ladies* for several seasons. But there always seem to be new young dancers coming along to take the places that the others have left. The company has a very loyal audience, black and white, who return year after year for the City Center season. Among the people who come to see that company are some who have never before seen dance as an art form. Some decide that they like what they see and go to performances of other companies as well.

Also, Ailey, perhaps more than any other choreographer, has made dance respectable among young boys and men. The strength, athletic ability and just plain masculine force of his male dancers are unmistakable.

CHAPTER XII

The Moderns: Martha Graham and Merce Cunningham

The early modern dancers were very serious. They decided that they did not want to entertain . . . they had a stricter attitude towards the audiences . . . Martha Graham at one time said that she went out on the stage with a whip in her hand to educate the audience not just to sit there and passively enjoy themselves. . . .

—DON MCDONAGH in *Contemporary Dance*

Merce Cunningham, I suspect, will always be controversial. At the very least, at any concert he gives, somebody, no doubt, will walk out in anger, or bafflement, or derision. There is in Cunningham's work an element of originality that never allows his audiences . . . to relax or to take him for granted. He is by nature a pioneer who from the start needed to find fresh answers to old questions, to create, rather than exploit or even inherit.

—DALE HARRIS in *Contemporary Dance*

W HILE, on ballet stages all over the United States, young
women were twirling on their toes and young men were leaping
gracefully and pirouetting in the air, dancers who looked very
different were showing us a whole new way of moving. They
were dancing to a different piper. For want of a better term, they
were called "modern dancers," which basically meant that their
roots were not in ballet, but in some other type of dance. Many
were influenced by Isadora Duncan, Ruth St. Denis and Ted
Shawn. Eventually, some would adapt a few ballet techniques to
their choreographies, although they never based their movements on classical ballet positions nor used toe shoes to allow
women performers to dance on point.

Of all those who invented new ways of expressing emotions
through new forms of dance, by far the most influential is Martha
Graham.

Born at the turn of the century, a tenth generation American
(she traces her ancestry back to Miles Standish), she was brought
up in California, and while in high school, determined to become
a dancer. Her father was a physician and in her solidly upper-
middle-class family dancing was probably not regarded as a suitable profession for a young lady. Nevertheless, she prevailed upon
her parents to allow her to study full time at the Denishawn
School in Los Angeles. She stayed at the school, eventually as a
member of the company, until 1923. Then she came to New York
City and got her first job dancing in a show called *The Greenwich
Village Follies* (which must really have shocked her parents).

These shows were a kind of variety entertainment with singers, jugglers, comedians, and other types of performers. Often
there was one so-called "art" spot, something that the manager
of the show considered "serious" or "artistic." Graham apparently filled that particular requirement in the *Follies*. It must
have been a generally unsatisfactory experience because she
never did anything like that again.

From then on, she performed on her own, sometimes with
other modern dancers and sometimes alone, in small concert
halls, studios, or wherever she could gather an audience. Since

her kind of movements were new to both audiences and reviewers, the notices she collected (when she was noticed at all) were not exactly enthusiastic. One dance writer recalled a review in a St. Louis paper in which it was suggested that Graham, during her performance, was either having an epileptic seizure or was giving birth to a baby. Another reviewer said that if she were giving birth, it probably was to a cube.

In the early 1930s, she decided to tour this country from New York to California and back. She played to small audiences and received very little attention from the dance press. When she returned, she found a letter from Joseph Goebbels, the propaganda minister of Nazi Germany, inviting her to dance at a special concert in conjunction with the 1936 Olympic games, which were scheduled for Berlin. All expenses for herself and her company, of course, would be paid by the German government, and she would be treated as an honored guest of the Third Reich.

Obviously, the offer must have been tempting. After all, in her own country there was apparently not one reviewer who had one kind word to say about her efforts. Nevertheless, she firmly turned down the invitation. "I don't think that I could possibly dance in your country where you don't even have respect for your own citizens. I don't see how you could have respect for foreign nationals, and besides, half my company would not be welcome in your country," she wrote in reply. Some members of her company were Jewish.

Although she publicized neither the invitation nor her firm rejection of it, someone in the American government must have heard the story and respected her for her stand. At any rate, she received a letter from the White House inviting her and one member of her company to dance for the President of the United States at a private party for state guests. She became the first American dancer to receive such an invitation. (Many years later, one of her students would occupy the White House as First Lady. That student was Betty Ford.) The invitation not only was an unprecedented honor, it also gave her career a much-needed boost. Potential audiences and reviewers seemed to think that if she was good enough to dance at the White House, she could not be as peculiar as they had thought her.

After her White House performance, her career definitely took an upward swing. She toured the United States again, this time to larger audiences and more sympathetic press coverage.

She toured Europe and the Middle East, where her dancing and her revolutionary choreographies were received enthusiastically. It is interesting to note that American modern dancers found their first audiences and critical acclaim not at home, but in Europe. The same had happened to Isadora Duncan, Ruth St. Denis and others.

Often Graham confused even those who liked her work. She changed her style and technique several times during her career. Just as her audience got accustomed to one new way of dancing, she had embarked on yet another. "For every new work, there was not only a new design in steps, but a new concept in technique and dynamics, a restudying of the basis of movement. No other choreographer has attempted so much," writes Agnes de Mille in her book, *America Dances.*

Many of Graham's choreographies told stories, often tragic tales of the fall of kings or of the trials and triumphs of men and women torn apart by a difficult fate. None of these stories was ever simple, the way the nineteenth-century ballets had been. What Graham was probing for were the deep feelings of love, hate, envy, frustration and joy in the heroes and heroines she portrayed. In a way, her choreographies were dance-dramas, with a meaning over and above the movements of the dancers.

From the first, her dance language was something that had not been seen before in this country. Agnes de Mille, who watched this development with appreciation and eagerness almost from the beginning, describes how Graham "threw aside all of the traditional steps and techniques of ballet: the straight long legs, the pointed toes, the quiet, even hips, the flexed foot, the relaxed hand." Instead Graham stressed "continuous, unfolding movement from a central core." As part of her choreography, she used the floor from which ballet dancers usually try to escape, either by dancing on point or by high and wide jumps. Instead Graham used falls and recoveries from falls. In other words, her dancers seemed thoroughly grounded, unlike ballet dancers who tend to look as if they are dancing on air. She also had her dancers balance on bent knees with their thighs as a hinge and the spine cantilevered and suspended backwards as a counterbalance, according to de Mille's description of one dance.

De Mille also points out that, although at first she seemed to be showing us dance techniques that we had not seen previously, and that to many of us seemed unintelligible, in reality her dance was far closer to natural acting than to ballet dancing. It was not a realistic imitation of emotion, as in acting, however; it was an imaginative expansion of acting. Children today who have not been trained in a balletic mold find her style sympathetic and easy to understand.

When Graham first performed her roles, many critics wrote that when she could no longer dance herself, her work could not possibly be performed by others. Whatever was happening on that stage depended entirely on this one dancer's magnetism and personality, they predicted. This has not turned out to be true. Graham, who is now in her eighties, has almost from the beginning run her own school. And the dancers who come from that school do her roles magnificently. There are usually some who sit in the audience and say sadly, "Well, that was all right, but you should have seen *Martha* dance it." But for those of us who have never seen Martha, nor ever will, what her company does is moving and extraordinary. Her choreographies have been taught by her to a group of talented students who understand what she is about, who will teach students in the next generation of dancers. The living chain that is required for a dance style or a choreography to continue beyond its originators has already been firmly established in the case of Martha Graham.

Among her story choreographies, those that are most easily understood are *Appalachian Spring* to the music of Aaron Copland, and *Clytemnestra* to the music of Halim El-Dabh.

Appalachian Spring, first performed in 1944, tells a very simple story of a young man and his bride, moving into their first home somewhere on the American frontier. The young woman is both happy and frightened at the prospects of her new life. One has the feeling, although the idea is never expressed directly, that she comes from a city, or at least an environment less primitive than the one to which she is now dedicating her life. She seeks reassurance from her obviously solid and loving husband, and from a character identified in the program only as "the Pioneer woman," a strongly maternal, protective and secure older female who seems to know both the joys and the many hardships the young bride can expect.

In the wedding party there is also a preacher, apparently one of those spellbinding hell-and-damnation clergymen who must have been seen frequently in the early days when America expanded her boundaries. He is accompanied by a group of "followers" who go into religious ecstasy every time the preacher shows his religious fervor. The young couple enter their new home. The preacher blesses it, and the pioneer woman shows the young bride that, in the uncertain future, she can be counted on as a friend. Everyone leaves the young couple alone in their new home with the bride sitting in a rocking chair and her husband standing firmly and lovingly behind her, his hand resting on her shoulder. The curtain falls.

What is so amazing about this choreography is that with a minimum of story content, it can give so profound a picture of the feelings of a young woman facing an uncertain future and deeply in love with the man she has married. The interdependence in the frontier community and the important part religion must have played in people's lives is never directly expressed, but it is indicated unmistakably nonetheless. Graham, with a few sparing gestures, manages to tell volumes. In this dance, a picture is indeed worth a thousand words.

Clytemnestra is an entirely different kind of story dance. The tale that is told is much more complicated and the emotions it evokes are much more mixed than the straightforward love and sympathy of *Appalachian Spring*. First given in 1958, the choreography tells the story in flashback of the life of a queen in ancient Greece. Clytemnestra was married to Agamemnon, the king of a Greek city-state. When the Trojan prince, Paris, seduces and then abducts Helen, wife of Agamemnon's brother, the Greeks go to war to get her back. The fleet is in the harbor ready to sail for Greece, but there is no wind. Agamemnon is told that if he sacrifices his daughter, Iphegenia, to the Gods, the wind will blow and the fleet will be able to sail. He sends messengers back to his castle to bring his daughter and her mother, Clytemnestra, to the harbor with a false story that the young woman is to be married to the greatest military hero of Greece, Achilles. When the two women arrive, they are appalled at the ambitious king's real plans. Clytemnestra begs her husband not to kill her child . . . after all, why should Helen be worth her daughter's life? But her pleas fall on deaf ears. The daughter is killed, and the fleet sails. Clytemnestra never forgives her husband for what he has done. When he is away, she takes a lover who, with her, rules the city-state. Her other daughter, Electra, however, never forgives her mother for her faithlessness to Agamemnon.

The audience sees all this as a flashback. By now Clytemnestra is dead and in Hades and is "dishonored even in the land of the dead," as the chorus sings. She is trying to remember what happened in her earthly life to cause this dishonor, and slowly, the pictures of that life emerge in her mind.

When Agamemnon returns, he is even more arrogant than when he left. Not only does he show no remorse for the killing of Iphegenia, but has brought along with him as his slave and mistress one of the Trojan king's daughters, the sister of Paris, Cassandra. He flaunts the younger woman in his wife's presence. She and her lover plot to kill Agamemnon, and they slay him with a sword.

Electra knows what has happened, and to avenge her father, persuades her brother Orestes to kill his mother and her lover. He does, and from then on is pursued by the Furies.

In her half-dream, half-wakened state in Hades, Clytemestra forgives Orestes for what he has done, and her soul is finally at peace.

This is a very brief summary of the story Graham tells us. It is, of course, a great deal more complicated than anything the classic ballets ever attempted. Not only does Graham give us the narrative, she also managed in her choreography to convey the emotions, tensions and conflicts in the minds of her many characters. The choreography, like *Appalachian Spring,* could not possibly have been made by any artist but Graham. She danced in both of these works herself, and *Clytemnestra* was one of the choreographies many critics believed depended entirely on her interpretation of the character. It has, however, been since danced by several of her students and the piece seems to have lost none of its emotional impact.

Both *Appalachian Spring* and *Clytemnestra* are part of public television's "Dance in America" series. They are rebroadcast usually once or twice a year. And, although seeing a dance on television cannot possibly be as interesting as seeing it live on stage, these two particular choreographies lend themselves especially well to TV. It is worth watching a program guide to see when they will be broadcast again and to make a point of viewing them.

MERCE CUNNINGHAM, one of Graham's most gifted students, is an entirely different kind of modern dancer and choreographer.

A native of Centralia, Washington, he studied tap, folk and exhibition ballroom dancing in his home town, performed locally in amateur shows and did a brief vaudeville and nightclub tour of Oregon and California before settling down to serious dance studies at Bennington College's Summer School of the Arts. There he was seen by Martha Graham and was invited to join her company. While working with Graham, he also studied ballet at the School of American Ballet and taught a class in modern dance at that school. He is, therefore, versed in almost every aspect of dance, but has developed a dancing and choreographic style that is uniquely his own.

He left Graham in 1944 and founded his own company and school in 1953. Since then he has worked closely with a number of modern composers, particularly John Cage, whose music sounds like nothing one may have heard before. It seems to have no melodic or even steady rhythmic line. Listening to it, one becomes involved in a system of sounds that often seem to have no central core, no recognizable beginning or end, except that the music starts and eventually stops. It fitted Cunningham's idea of dance perfectly.

He feels that music and dance are entirely separate entities, perhaps working side by side, but not necessarily together. So, one of his dances may seem to have very little to do with the music that is played during it. The only contact of the two arts is that when the music starts the dancers begin to dance, and when the music stops, the dancers also stop.

Cunningham is difficult to understand, both as a dancer and as a person. Sometimes one finds oneself completely caught up in one of his choreographies without knowing exactly why. At other times, that same choreography can seem only confusing.

One writer who apparently knows him well, Moira Hodgson, describes him like this: "Cunningham is reclusive, maintaining his distance from his dancers. He rarely praises or flatters, never explains a movement but leaves them to find it in their own bodies. He reveals little about himself. He has a powerful stage presence, and can hold an audience simply by sitting in a chair and doing absolutely nothing. He moves like an animal, with no effort or tension, with the tranquility of a yogi. At times his movements look so natural he does not appear to be dancing. These days he performs less with the dancers, concentrating on solos. His dances for the rest of the company contain more unison than before, most of it extremly demanding."

Cunningham's dancers often look as if they were improvising, which, of course, they are not. But he does not like his pieces to look choreographed. Members of his company must be excellent dancers because, when one watches them closely, it becomes obvious that what they are doing is very difficult. But they are never what he calls "flashy:" they do little jumping and spinning. Their movements are often slow and deliberate. What they seem to need most of all is superb muscle control and balance. When Cunningham wants his dancers to get from one spot to another, he rarely has them run or jump, they walk instead. He doesn't like his dancers to look comfortable in their positions either. "I think dance only comes alive when it gets awkward again," he says.

Cunningham still performs himself. Nobody seems to know exactly how old he is, but just looking at the dates of his choreographies, one has to come to the conclusion that he must be about seventy. There is no way to tell his age from his dancing. He usually looks as strong as the young members of his company.

Whether the Cunningham repertory will survive as Martha Graham's undoubtedly will is a question. His style is so individual and so difficult to communicate to other dancers that many of his works may not be transferable to a successor. But meanwhile, what he has done is unique and has had an influence on many other modern dancers who have adapted what he has taught them to their own particular styles and repertory. Because he has been able to carry certain dance principles further than any other choreographer before him wished or was able to do, he will remain a major force in American dance history.

CHAPTER XIII

More Moderns: Paul Taylor and Twyla Tharp

If other people want to analyze what I do, that's fine with me . . . but I won't. It has too much to do with instinct, feelings, your personal experience in dance and outside it. It is life. It is much too mysterious to begin to understand.

PAUL TAYLOR in *Quintet* by Moira Hodgson

. . . Twyla Tharp seems to be moving towards a new quality of plain speech in classical choreography. At times she seems to be on the verge of creating a new style, a new humanity for classical ballet and ballet dancers . . . . It's amazing to think what a promoter like Diaghilev would have done with her . . . he would proclaim 'la Tharp' the herald of a new age. Which she is.

—ARLENE CROCE in her book *After-Images*, reviewing a choreography by Twyla Tharp called *As Time Goes By.*

THE KINDS of dances created by choreographers Paul Taylor and Twyla Tharp are very different from each other. The styles and shapes of their dancers are different. But the audiences are similar: young. It's obvious that these choreographers are developing the dance audiences and patrons of the future. Indeed, at a Tharp performance, which in New York City usually takes place in a Broadway theater, anyone over the age of thirty might well feel self-conscious.

There are reasons why these two choreographers, so different in their approach to dance, appeal to the young. There is a noticeable lack of pretension, of deliberate artiness, of attempts to create something vaguely "cultural" in their work. Both choreographers also have young companies that radiate speed, confidence and enthusiasm. Taylor has invented a word for the quality he feels his dancers must have: "zunch." What he means by that is a little difficult to define; indeed, if it were possible to define it exactly, he probably would not have needed to coin a new term. Taylor himself has a variety of explanations but one definition he gave recently seems to cover the meaning: "Zunch is what sets an exciting dancer apart from an average one. It is the magic that stays with the viewer after the dance is finished. It is the ability of the dancer to focus on what may be a tiny gesture and to hurl it from one soul to another. It can be that extra little push that makes a leap only a fraction of an inch higher, but astonishes the audience because it clearly comes from the dancer's total courage and commitment. It is what your favorite dancers do to allow you to see their special and mysterious human values."

Today's young dance audiences obviously love "zunch" whether they see it in the Taylor or the Tharp companies.

Both Taylor and Tharp were superb dancers themselves a few years ago. Both have now stopped dancing and are choreographing and managing their own companies full time. Taylor, who was a member of Martha Graham's company for many years, danced in a work *Episodes* in 1959 in which Graham collaborated with Balanchine. The Taylor solo was made by Balanchine. The New York City Ballet still has *Episodes* in its repertory, but the

Taylor solo has been eliminated from the current version. Apparently nobody else can dance it to Balanchine's exacting standards.

Taylor was born in Pittsburgh, Pennsylvania, and like many modern dancers came to his profession relatively late. He attended Syracuse University on a scholarship for painting, and while there became a champion swimmer, before transferring to the Juilliard School of Music's dance department. He went to an audition with virtually no previous dance training and was accepted on a scholarship. Eventually, he danced with both the Graham and the Cunningham companies.

He formed his own group in 1956, which, like so many top American dance companies, was first acclaimed in Europe. He still tours Europe and South America, gives a short New York City season and appears on many college campuses throughout the United States. Occasionally, another company will adopt one of the pieces in his repertory. The American Ballet Theater, for instance, now does *Airs*, a lovely dance to music by Handel. Although the choreography does not use standard ballet techniques, with both men and women dancing barefoot, the dance works almost as well with the young dancers of the ABT as it does in Taylor's own company. When *Airs* was cast by ABT, care was obviously taken to find dancers who could master Taylor's difficult jumps and perform at his speed. Those involved in the enterprise were young corps members who apparently had more zunch than the older, more experienced dancers.

Taylor uses baroque music exceedingly well, unlike many of his fellow modern choreographers, who prefer music composed in the twentieth century. The piece that has become the signature dance for the company is *Esplanade*, made to the Double Violin Concerto by Bach. Balanchine used this same music to choreograph a piece he called *Concerto Barocco*. It's fascinating to observe how differently the two choreographers treated the composition. Balanchine's work is full of delicacy, emphasizing the careful counterpoint construction of the piece. Taylor emphasized speed and exuberance. In the Taylor version, the dancers' movements are all natural . . . they jump, walk and run. Often they suddenly shift directions, seemingly changing their minds about where to go next in the middle of the stage. "This particular Bach composition pulled me in very unexpected directions," Taylor has said, echoing in words what his dancers do on stage. "It is very strange . . . when you listen to the music, it sounds so symmetrical. But when you start working with it, it is full of uneven counts, regroupings and shifting tempos." Musicians have said that about Bach for generations. And the fact that the music often turns out to be so unexpected apparently has frightened choreographers away from it. There are few choreographies to Bach by anyone, and the two most successful are to the same composition, by Balanchine and Taylor.

Taylor has also done a few semi-story choreographies. Although they apparently tell us some kind of tale, it is never entirely clear exactly what is meant. For instance, a dance called *Big Bertha* shows a family at an outdoor amusement park with the figure of the Big Bertha as a sort of slot machine. The family, which in the beginning looks like an average American Mom, Pop and kid, falls apart during the course of the dance. The Big Bertha figure, at first a standard amusing carnival exhibit, becomes more and more menacing. The ending is bloody and brutal. What is Taylor trying to tell us? That our amusements can brutalize us? That at the root of every family there is potential hatred and violence, as well as love and caring? That nothing is really what it seems? Whatever he is saying is not explained in the program notes, and reviewers have interpreted the piece in dozens of different ways. Basically, one's view of the piece comes down to what dancer-choreographer Peter Martins said about one of his own pieces: "You see what you think you see."

Another piece, *From Sea to Shining Sea*, is clearly a satiric comment on much of what many believe about America. The characters include a Pilgrim who lands at Plymouth Rock and who punches the friendly Indian who welcomes him in the nose; housewives with hair curlers who brush their teeth on stage; Mickey Mouse and a Statue of Liberty that turns into a Ku Klux Klansman. The piece, at the end, is bitter rather than funny. One wants to compare it to a Balanchine ballet, *Stars and Stripes*, which, to Sousa marches, has corps members twirling batons, kicking up their heels, and doing the kinds of formations that pom-pom girls often do at football games. Balanchine has a male dancer who portrays Uncle Sam and a woman who is called Liberty Belle. The dances he has given the two soloists are not only acrobatically very difficult, they are also genuinely funny. But one feels that Balanchine is smiling at America, that his satire is loving as well as amusing. Taylor's is not loving—it's angry. Both choreographies are distinguished, however, and will probably be performed for many decades to come.

Taylor's dancers all have distinct, individual personalities, which show on stage. Unlike the dancers in most other groups, they don't look as if they all came off one particular assembly line. They can be tall or short, pretty or not so pretty, handsome or not so handsome, square, thin and in between. Of course, none of them is fat. But, one feels that if it were possible, Taylor might one day include someone who weighed 200 pounds, just to see how he or she would work with the company. What's more, Taylor, unlike any other choreographer, encourages his dancers to *show* their own individuality on stage. He expects them to act like persons, rather than as members of a group . . . although, of course, he also expects them to stay in time with the music and to follow the choreography.

OUT OF THIS assorted group came one supremely talented woman who formed her own company, unofficially, with a recital of a piece called *Tank Dive* in Room 1604 of the Hunter College Art Department. Since then Twyla Tharp has choreographed over fifty pieces for her own group, two for ABT, two for the Joffrey Ballet, and was the choreographer as well as, with her entire company, among the dancers in the film version (not the Broadway musical) of *Hair*.

Tharp seems challenged by innovative assignments. She made a special choreography for champion skater John Curry and has choreographed pieces especially for television that look very different from the usual dances that are done on a stage and then simply photographed by TV cameras. She adapted her pieces to the kinds of technology TV has available, that the stage and even films do not. She used double images, enlarged some dancers to cover the whole screen while having others reduced to dancing in a tiny space somewhere in the right or left corner, for instance. In a way, what she has been able to do with television techniques is probably prophetic: dance will be seen more and more on television in the years to come and will develop in new directions. In fact, like all entertainment, the future of dance may lie in what television can do with it, so choreographies will change to suit the new technologies. Tharp saw this several years ago . . . before anyone else did.

She also saw dance movements in sports and choreographed,

again for television, a piece that contrasted the New York City Ballet's Peter Martins with Lynn Swann of the Pittsburgh Steelers. It was amazing how the movements of the two men were similar in many ways and contrasted in others.

A tall, long-legged dancer with short straight hair, she was born and grew up in Indiana. Twyla Tharp, stagy as it sounds, is her *real* name. It seems that her mother particularly admired a champion hog caller called "Twyla" and named her daughter after the woman. For some reason the name seems to suit her. She looks and talks like a Twyla Tharp: sharp, witty, lively, self-confident, and as one of her coworkers puts it: "She has a gift for success." She also has an unmistakable gift for choreography, and even a piece that at first glance seems light and flippant always has a serious core of careful construction and attention to the music.

If there is such a thing as a hit ballet, Tharp has produced it: *Push Comes to Shove*, to a musical score that combines ragtime with Haydn, was made for the American Ballet Theater and Baryshnikov. It brings down the house at every performance and has been scheduled at least ten times in every one of ABT's New York seasons for the past five years. Baryshnikov is the only one who dances the principal role. He has no understudy for the part. If, for any reason, he is unable to perform, the ballet is cancelled and rescheduled at a later date.

This is what he has to say about that choreography: "*Push Comes To Shove* is a 'tour de force.' It is so meticulously constructed, so technically perfect. If you watch it carefully, you see the seriousness of the intent. Many people say that Twyla gives you what you want. Well, she does, but her work springs from a complete dedication of an idea. In *Push*, for example, the balance between two kinds of music. The rag, with its jazzy upbeat is so skillfully attached to the Haydn that one comes to think, 'well, yes, of course, that's the way it *has* to be'."

He obviously enjoys dancing the piece. It brings out the many facets of his personality, his sense of humor, his ability to switch dancing styles in split seconds, as well as requiring every bit of his unusual classical dance skills. In *Push Comes to Shove*, Baryshnikov can be Charlie Chaplin, Fred Astaire, a clown in a Russian circus and the superb classical dancer we usually see when he dances. Obviously, Tharp studied *him* before she did the piece almost as thoroughly as she studied the music.

She did a second piece for an ABT gala in which she actually danced with Baryshnikov. It was called *Once More Frank*, and was choreographed to a series of Frank Sinatra recorded songs. About that piece, Baryshnikov says: "The dance was about Twyla and Misha, the dancers, working out a specific dance problem: how two dancers with such different backgrounds and styles and techniques can find a middle ground, a performing style that sustains both of them."

Her ballet, *Douce Coupe*, to a recording of a Beach Boys' concert (one hears the cheering fans and some of the musicians' patter in the particular tape that is used for the performances), was made for the Joffrey. Initially, it was a way of contrasting ballet style with other dance styles including disco, jitterbug and jazz. The work has been redone several times with less emphasis on those contrasts, and now just looks like a particularly lively, jazzy dance for a group of young performers.

Occasionally, Tharp decides that she wants to choreograph something that offers a social commentary on life in the United States. Recently she did two pieces that, essentially, comment on the breakdown of the American family: *When We Were Very Young*, in 1980, and in 1981, *The Catherine Wheel*.

Both works are at their best when she allows her dancers just to dance. Particularly in *The Catherine Wheel*, one sometimes gets the idea that it might have been better if Tharp allowed sociologists to practice sociology and concentrated on movements to music. The work divides clearly into two parts: the family breakdown, done mainly in black and white, and a pure dance number at the end with everyone in gold costumes. It's all done to the music of David Byrne of the rock group The Talking Heads. The black and white sections are murky, difficult to understand and, for Tharp, even dull. The gold section is glorious.

As dance critic, Arlene Croce, once said: "I never like dance pieces that try to make me think about philosophy." Tharp is at her best when she is thinking about music and the particular capacities of the dancers for whom she choreographs. As a social critic, she is often superficial and facile . . . as someone who makes dancers move, she is fascinating.

It is indeed becoming obvious
that American dancers are
turning out to be the best
in the world. In 1982, a relatively
unknown seventeen-year-old dancer
from the Washington, D.C. Ballet
won the Gold Medal at the Moscow
International Ballet Competition,
the first American so honored.

Here Amanda McKerrow
is learning a new ballet
from Choo San Goh,
a choreographer who, in
recent years, has done work
for the Washington Company
as well as the American Ballet
Theater, the Ailey Company
and the Paris Opera Ballet.

The sensation of the 1982 NYCB
season was a sixteen-year-old
dancer, Darci Kistler. She performed
in many major roles usually reserved
for much more experienced dancers.

Gelsey Kirkland is not trying
to see if she has a hole
in her slipper.
She is loosening up her muscles
in a standard ballet warm-up.

Dancers have to look wonderful
in very simple costumes,
like tight black tunics.
Karin Von Aroldingen
(here with Bart Cook) does.

*All these would-be ballerinas
are students at the School of
American Ballet, dancing **Swan Lake**
in the annual school production.*

*They also have to look lovely
and romantic in floating blue chiffon.
Karin Von Aroldingen again . . .
this time with Sean Lavery.*

3 A Dancer's Education and Life

CHAPTER XIV

Learning to Dance

Freedom for a dancer means only one thing . . . discipline.

—Dancer MARTHA GRAHAM

First comes the sweat; then comes the beauty.

—Choreographer GEORGE BALANCHINE, quoted in *Time.*

And what is so nice is that the students are so sweet to each other. No movie rages. It's all very agreeable.

—LINCOLN KIRSTEIN
President of the American School of Ballet, quoted in an interview in *The New York Times.*

THE DISCIPLINE is there and the sweat. The students are not only remarkably kind to each other, they are also polite and respectful to their teachers. Indeed, the top ballet school in the world may be the last bastion of what sometimes looks like Victorian good manners. Much of the youth culture of the nineteen-sixties, seventies and eighties seems to have passed it by. Everybody works incredibly hard. Drugs and alcohol don't seem to be problems there. An ice cream soda on a hot day or a cup of hot chocolate on a frigid one are considered to be great indulgences. Students don't curtsy or bow to teachers any more, as they did fifty years ago, but they do hold doors open for them. If they are corrected in class, they thank their instructor. There are few raised voices, no arguments in the halls. Everybody is on time for class.

Teachers in top dance schools have all been dancers themselves. They know how the pressures to excel and compete can wreck the best of dispositions. This has always been true in dance. So, although no one who teaches at one of the schools that prepares students for professional careers in dance has probably ever taken a course in educational psychology, the instructors know instinctively what they must teach their students from the beginning: a certain kind of consideration, concern, "a sweetness" towards each other. It is as much a part of the dance tradition as the steps and positions everybody practices, day after day at the barre.

Serious dance students know what is expected of them, and that unless they meet these expectations, they will not stay in whatever school they attend, no matter how much promise they show. In fact, even those who try as hard as they can may be dropped for reasons that have nothing to do with their efforts or attitudes. If, as they grow into adolescence, their body configurations turn out to be wrong for a dancer, if they do not meet certain exacting requirements, they will be told, kindly but firmly, that they should try some other profession.

There are literally thousands of dance schools in the world. In the United States there are a few in almost every middle-sized city and many in most large cities. Most of these schools don't take life in general, and dance in particular, all that seriously. They aren't there to prepare students for dance careers. They teach ballet, along with tap, jazz and disco as a form of healthy diversion. Students who wish to become *professional* dancers do not usually spend many years in such a school. By the time they are twelve or thirteen, they and their parents usually learn that in order to qualify for a place in a good dance company, they will have to study full-time at one of the few top schools in the country.

Most of the traditions of these schools, those for ballet at any rate, originated at the Imperial Ballet School in St. Petersburg, and many of the older and most revered teachers today are still graduates of that school, carrying its traditions as well as its techniques to their present teaching posts. Even in Russia, that school, which is affiliated with the Kirov Ballet, still trains the best of the Russian dancers, including those who have left their country for Europe and the United States: Rudolf Nureyev, Natalia Makarova and Mikhail Baryshnikov, for instance. The Kirov School may represent one of the few aspects of Russian life that has remained almost unchanged. The children are taught there just as they were 100 years ago, the same techniques and manners as other dance students all over the world. They have some courses in Communist history and ideology, but, according to most of the Russian dancers who have come to the West, these courses are taken seriously only by the bureaucrats who administer the school. They are regarded as time-consuming nuisances by most of the students. Somehow, most dancers are not very political, no matter what their country of origin.

Dancers leave Russia for some of the same reasons that others leave Denmark or France: they want to dance with a particular company or in a particular style that is not available to them in their own country.

Most European countries, like Russia, have official dance academies, affiliated with national ballet companies and financed by the government. In Russia and in several European countries, dance students live in dormitories and go to special schools to learn academic skills along with their dance classes. All of this is free, as are the leotards, dance slippers and other gear required for dancing. There is, of course, also free medical and dental care for the youngsters and often they are also provided with some pocket money by the state.

None of this is true in the United States. We have no government-supported dance academies, as we have no official ballet companies. But today, the school that is generally regarded to be the best ballet school in the world is in the United States: The School of American Ballet, housed inconspicuously on the second floor of the Juilliard School of Music, Lincoln Center, New York City.

Every year, thousands of boys and girls from this country and abroad apply to this school. During the very early years (usually starting at age six to about eight), the children who come are usually residents of New York City and its suburbs. At that point, the selection process is not too strict, although everyone is required to pass some kind of audition.

The process of picking promising students becomes really serious at the intermediate level when the youngsters are twelve or thirteen years old. Then those seeking entrance, or those already there who do not measure up, are told, gently but firmly, that the school is for *professionals* and that, if a child has little chance to become a professional dancer, the School of American Ballet is not the place to be. Teachers know that some children and parents will be deeply disappointed by such judgments, but they also know that the hurt would be much deeper if students were allowed to continue working, year after year, with no hope of ever making it in the highly competitive dance world.

By the time the students who are accepted have reached adolescence, most of them are taking dance classes full time. They attend the Professional Children's School in New York City for a few hours a day, but most of their days are spent at the school learning everything from basic ballet to other types of dance, mime, make-up, and other stage skills. They are preparing themselves for a specific profession, the way a law student prepares to be an attorney, a medical student to be a physician, and someone in teacher's college to be an educator. The difference, of course, is that dancers have made their vocational choice much earlier.

By the time students have reached their middle teens, many are no longer from New York City. Every year the School of American Ballet holds auditions all over the country to select the most promising applicants from the best local and regional dance schools. Some are invited to come to New York City for a summer session of the School of American Ballet. If they seem to have the talent and drive to make a full-time course worthwhile, they are asked to come back as regular students during the school year. Many of these out-of-town youngsters live in approved boarding homes, often run by former dancers. Some of the older ones share apartments near Lincoln Center. Thanks to a large Ford Foundation grant, the School is able to offer scholarships to those promising applicants who cannot afford to pay tuition. Some also receive a stipend for living expenses. But, in the United States, educating a future dancer may be almost as expensive for a family as educating a future lawyer or college professor.

The teachers at the school are almost always dancers who

are now, or have been in the past, associated with Balanchine and the New York City Ballet. Some of these teachers also spend time traveling around the country to hold auditions for would-be dancers, who may be asked to come to New York for the tryout summer session.

One of those who picks students and teaches a regular course at the School is one of New York City Ballet's principal dancers, Karin von Aroldingen. She is one of the few women in the company who received her early dance education not at the School of American Ballet, but in Europe, and is therefore, familiar with European standards and teaching methods as well as American ones. She studied ballet in Germany, was a principal dancer with the Berlin Ballet at eighteen, and came to the United States when Balanchine saw her and asked her to join his company, where she started as a corps member although she had already been an important soloist in Europe. What does she look for in a potential student?

"Not technical ability," she says. "That's what our school will help them to achieve. I look at the body first. It should be lean, with good proportions, longish legs, a long neck and fairly small head. But a good body is not enough. There has to be some special quality . . . something to make that young person interesting. Even a dancer with a beautiful body can be boring.

"Sometimes, when I go to a place to audition there are at least sixty youngsters who want me to look at them. Obviously, you can't really *see* that many at once. So I take them in groups of twenty, and concentrate on those who seem promising. I ask them to point their feet to see if they are flexible. I ask them to raise their legs to see if they can achieve the turned-out quality a dancer needs. Then I often ask a few to come back so I can talk to them and find out a little about their personalities and attitudes. A student must really want to be a dancer on her own. If she has a mother who wants her to be a dancer, but she would just as soon do something entirely different, the time to find that out is before we start her at the school. The discipline and the work there are so hard and demanding that unless a student is motivated, he or she will simply be miserable and drop out. That's hard on them and a waste of time and resources for us."

Von Aroldingen is married and has a teen-age daughter who, incidentally, does not want to be a dancer. Von Aroldingen knows how difficult it is for a young woman to combine ballet with marriage and motherhood and will answer honestly questions about this problem, which some teen-age girls ask before they make up their minds whether or not to devote themselves seriously to ballet. For instance, although many of the women in the company are married, few have children, and those who become pregnant often decide to leave. Von Aroldingen did not leave. She danced until she was several months into her pregnancy. ("I was lucky . . . I did not show for several months," she says.) She resumed her career quickly after her child was born. But, again, she is an exception, and she will tell young would-be dancers that ballet can indeed take over one's whole life.

According to her experience, if a girl or boy really wants to be a dancer, he or she already knows that life won't be easy or glamorous. "Most of them have read enough about dance or know some people who are dancers so that they are aware of the difficulties as well as the joys," she says. "They have already thought through all the problems they might face and decided to take their chances. Those kids who come to New York as teenagers to attend our school are often amazingly mature. They know what they want; they know they are taking a chance; and they are willing to do what is necessary."

Actually, von Aroldingen would like to see teen-age dance students take more interest in something other than dancing. "I would like to see them read more, learn more," she says. "Often, even with the best possible instincts, it is not possible to predict how a boy or a girl will develop. Some can look terrific at fifteen, and then suddenly, at sixteen, grow in ways that make the body no longer suitable for ballet. Mothers ask me if they should allow their fifteen-year-old daughters to drop out of school altogether so they can dance. I discourage that whenever possible. Dancing is a fragile career. It's important to have other intellectual and emotional resources."

One of the advantages that the School of American Ballet offers to some of its students is early stage experience. Many of Balanchine's ballets include children: *The Nutcracker* in which two children play the principal roles and there are corps roles for many other youngsters; *Coppelia, Midsummer Night's Dream* and *Harlequinade*, all with dozens of youngsters in the cast. They don't function as spear-carrying extras either. They *dance*. So children learn about rehearsal schedules, which take up much of their spare time, disappointments when someone has to be

134

eliminated from a role, and even stage fright. The youngsters used in these ballets often start at a very young age. In *Nutcracker*, for instance, there are children as young as six. There are fewer roles for older students in actual stage productions.

The critical point in the lives of young dancers is the annual student performance, given in the spring with a full orchestra, scenery, costumes and a sold-out auditorium. The audience is not made up entirely (or even largely) of admiring parents, friends and relatives. There are the critics from all the New York newspapers and magazines that review regular ballet performances in New York. There are scouts from other companies, which often hire graduates who do not make it into the New York City Ballet. And there are all those balletomanes who enjoy spotting future stars among the ranks of students during these performances.

Obviously, not all graduates of the School can be absorbed into the New York City Ballet, although that seems to be everyone's first choice. In the top classes, the real competition is among those who might make it into the Company. For instance, when she was a graduating student dancer, Antonia Franceschi played a leading role in the movie *Fame*, a story about the New York High School for Performing Arts. As a result, she was offered a motion picture contract that would have paid in one year probably as much as she can make as a ballet dancer in ten years. She chose to decline the contract offer and to join the New York City Ballet as an apprentice for one year. In 1982, she became a regular member of the corps, although she had already danced solo roles in other dance companies during the summer.

Often, by the time a student is ready to graduate, outstanding talent is obvious. The year a young dancer, Darci Kistler, now a soloist with the New York City Ballet, appeared in a short version of *Swan Lake* as the Swan Queen in a student production, the atmosphere in the audience was electric. Apparently almost everyone there already had heard of the spectacular fifteen-year-old. It is always difficult to buy a ticket for that student performance, but the year in which Darci danced as a member of the graduating class, tickets were almost impossible to obtain. Even reviewers, who usually are given two seats, that year got only one.

Of course, the School of American Ballet is the only *one* ballet school. There are others in New York as well as in almost any major city in the United States. There are schools in Europe, in South America, and now even in China. But countries that have their own national dance academies are now hiring graduates of the School of American Ballet. Looking over a program of the Stuttgart Ballet, Germany's best company, one can see many clearly American first and last names. The first conclusion that one might reach is that, as formerly American dancers adopted Russian names in order to make it in this country, now Germans are adopting American names. Not true. Almost all those dancers were graduates of the New York City School. And Stuttgart has a school of its own attached to the company.

Some national companies in other countries are permitted by law to accept only citizens of their own countries as permanent members. But even then, some of those dancers have studied in the United States, usually at the School of American Ballet. American dancers, or dancers trained in America, are now at the forefront of ballet and modern dance all over the world. And looking at the 1982 student production of the School of American Ballet, it seems as if the situation is destined to continue for many years to come.

For those who want to be professional dancers in areas of dance other than ballet, the picture is not very different. Long years of study and good instruction are required to achieve the stamina and the technique to succeed, although in some other areas of dance, it is not necessary that students begin quite so young as in ballet. Once the process has begun, however, whether it is ballet, or the schools of modern dance started by Martha Graham or Alvin Ailey or Paul Taylor or whoever it may be, or for that matter if people want to succeed as tap dancers or jazz dancers, classes, long hours of meticulous practice and complete dedication to one's chosen profession, often to the exclusion of almost everything else, are required.

CHAPTER XV

A Dancer's Life

Dancers have always moved in an aura curious and provocative, if often at the same time despised. They are widely discriminated against, although their appeal at the moment seems to be universal. The figure of a ballet girl is constant in advertising, but laws and social customs are slow to reflect this enthusiasm. Dancers still cannot get leases or insurance as readily as other people, and in England they are not permitted to rent cars. The theater itself discriminates against them, and distinctions are made in dressing rooms, courtesies and comforts, fees and billings. A dancer who wishes to better his terms materially must become an actor at even the cost of subordinating his true métier [profession]. This still pertains in an age when dancers break historical frontiers and set standards unmatched before. How hard do bad traditions die.

—American choreographer AGNES DE MILLE
in *To a Young Dancer*

A SEVENTEEN-YEAR-OLD BALLET DANCER was sitting at a table in a small dinette near New York's Lincoln Center with several other dancers. All were slowly sipping diet sodas. They chose that particular drink because it had no calories and dancers have to watch their weight more carefully than members of any other profession, including models. They were taking their time because the owner of the dinette looks unkindly on customers who are not actively engaged in eating and drinking while continuing to occupy a table.

The dancer needed a cool place to sit for a while. The temperature outside was a humid ninety degrees, and everybody's muscles ached, as usual. They had just come from an especially demanding audition, an "open call" for the corps de ballet at the American Ballet Theater.

An open call means that all who consider themselves qualified can appear. However, not everybody is allowed to show what he or she can do. At the ABT call, more than 400 dancers showed up to compete for ten places in the corps. More than half were eliminated before they even had a chance to put on their slippers, by a so-called "body cut." That means that the ballet master looked at them and decided, after one fast glance, that they were the wrong shape or size for his particular company. Two hundred dancers were sent home before the audition even began. The rest were put through their paces in groups of ten. Then about fifty were allowed to show what they could do, for about five minutes each, in groups of four. Of these, twenty were selected to return the next day for a final workout and, each one hoped, a spot in the company.

Of the four dancers sitting at the table, only seventeen-year-old Joan had been called back. This was the most important audition she had attended in her life—and she was understandably elated and excited. She knew she had only a fifty-fifty chance of being one of the ten new ABT members—but she was hopeful. "I know I'm talented," she said. "I've been on dance scholarships ever since I was ten years old. I went to the best ballet school in the world. I work terribly hard . . . and I keep my weight down. My mother thinks I'm much too thin. She keeps telling me I look like one of those wartime refugees. But ballet masters like thin girls. It's really time I got a job. I can't hold out much longer. My folks think I should go to secretarial school or something . . ."

Joan has a great deal invested in her career, more than almost any other seventeen-year old who is not also a dancer. She started lessons in ballet in her home town, Dallas, Texas, at the age of six. From once-a-week lessons she had gone to three lessons per week by the time she was eight. When she was ten, she was going to dance class every day. During her twelfth year, a staff member of the School of American Ballet came through town to audition promising youngsters for the School's summer scholarship program. Joan was picked and spent the summer in New York, staying with family friends. She was asked to return the following year. At the end of that summer she was offered a full-time scholarship at the school. She was then fourteen years old, still very young to live away from her family. And the friends who had been so accommodating during the summer really could not be asked to take over Joan's room and board on a permanent basis. So she moved into a boarding house for dance students, run by the wife of a well-known dancer. She attended ballet school classes five to six hours a day and got what academic training she could at the Professional Children's School, a unique New York institution that provides the legally required courses in reading, writing, math and such subjects at odd hours for youngsters who work in the movies, TV, theater or dance during the times when other children go to school. So, during the years when most girls spend time with family and friends, go to movies, watch TV, play sports and pursue hobbies, Joan worked almost constantly.

"I hardly know anybody who is not a dancer," she says. "Nobody else works the crazy hours I do." Although she is outstandingly attractive, she has never had a real date. "The only boys I meet are also dancers," she adds. "They have as little time, and probably less money, than I do. When we go out, we usually go in a group . . . like now. We can't eat a lot, so restaurant meals would be out even if we could afford them. We are not allowed to roller skate, or play tennis, or ski, or participate in any sport that might cause an injury. Sometimes we go to the beach or to a pool to swim. Our teachers tell us swimming is the only sport that's really good for dancers. But even then we have to watch it. If there is too much surf, we are supposed to stay out of the water. A wave might knock us down. Also, we are not supposed to get tanned or sunburned. Somehow a tan does not look right on stage."

At seventeen, Joan is already worried that she is getting "too old" to continue looking for work in her chosen field for which she has sacrificed so much. Dancing is a young person's art. Most top dancers are performing regularly by the time they are sixteen or seventeen. By the time they reach forty, especially if their field is ballet, their careers are generally nearing the end. Ballet takes a serious toll on backs, knees and feet. As long as bodies are flexible (and that means young), they can usually withstand the demands of this most rigorous of all art forms. But once muscles and joints begin to wear out, injuries multiply, and eventually, dancing becomes not only too painful, but impossible.

Still Joan has no idea what she would do if she did not dance. It's the only profession she has ever considered. "There are mornings when I get out of bed and all my muscles are so sore and stiff that I can hardly move. The idea of even the simplest warm-up exercise makes me want to turn over and go back to sleep. But I get up and take a hot shower. Then I start warm-ups, and after a few minutes, I hurt less. By the time I get to class, I'm fine. Of course, by evening everything hurts again, and then I do the whole routine all over again the next morning," she says. "But then I get to do a performance and everything comes together. Last year I danced several roles with a small company in Texas. When I am on stage, I suddenly stop hurting . . . and I also stop worrying about the future. I'd rather dance than do anything in the world. If someone offered me a million dollars to stop dancing, I probably would turn it down . . . well half a million anyway."

The chances that Joan, even if she is as successful as she hopes to be, will ever have a million dollars (or even half a million) are exceedingly dim. As Agnes de Mille points out, dancers are not paid very much. In fact, except for a half-dozen superstars, they make less money than people who move the furniture around on stage or even those who sew and take care of their costumes. They certainly do not earn the same salaries or receive the kind of job security that musicians in the orchestra receive. The reason for that is simple: most other workers associated with dance, music, theater, TV or movies belong to unions. Most dancers do not . . . although several years ago the corps members of ABT did join a union and demanded a living wage. They got locked out of their rehearsal and classrooms for several months as a result of their efforts, and one season was cancelled by the company, which meant that the dancers not only lost their salaries, but their rehearsal and practice space. Eventually, they got a fairer contract.

What were the dancers who were clearly among the most talented in their profession receiving before the union made its demands? Beginning dancers received $235 per week, often for seventy hours of work with no overtime. A soloist who had been with the company for ten years got $422 per week . . . also with no overtime. The season ran thirty-six weeks per year. There were no paid vacations, or holidays. When the company was not dancing, everybody went on unemployment insurance.

What finally toughened the bargaining stance of the dancers was the fact that the company allowed them only thirty dollars per day for expenses (including hotel and all meals) when they danced away from New York, and the company was away from New York for at least half the season. "Nobody could live on that . . . not even if we slept four to a room," one of the dancers in a picket line at Lincoln Center said. "We had to use our own money to pay for rooms and to eat. Of course, we also had to keep our New York apartments. That meant almost all of us had to ask our families for help. We were not making enough to survive, even though we worked seventy or eighty hours a week."

The company offered the corps members increases that totaled, for all of them, about $150,000 over a three-year-contract period. Management insisted that, like all ballet companies, they were operating in the red. Then the story broke about the Russian dancer, Aleksandr Godunov, who had defected with considerable publicity from Russia's Bolshoi Ballet, being hired by ABT at one hundred fifty thousand dollars for *one year*. At that point, the corps' members rebelled, probably for the first time in ballet history.

It took a while, but eventually they received a contract that specified better salaries and working conditions. The starting salary for a corps member is now $420 per week, and after ten years, a dancer will make a minimum of $610. The company will pay for hotel rooms, no matter what they cost (recently the cost of a modest hotel room in Washington, D.C., where the company dances for several weeks each year was eighty-five dollars per night), and will, in addition, contribute twenty dollars per day for meals. That's still not very much. Most dancers find that they cannot eat in restaurants the kind of low calorie, high nutrition food they must have to stay in shape. Many eat a container of yogurt for breakfast in their rooms and buy fruit and cheese for backstage lunches in order to stay within their budgets. But at least they no longer have to subsidize the company. Of course, they still don't get any paid vacations or holidays, and they still go on unemployment pay for several months a year.

Nor do their expenses stop when they are not performing. Almost all dancers take class in addition to what is offered by the company. For this they pay up to thirty dollars an hour. They almost all require massages, since that is one way tight muscles can be relaxed and potential injuries avoided. If they are seriously injured, their health insurance will take care of expenses. But for relatively minor ailments—sprains, stretched or inflamed tendons, bruises and cuts—they pay their own medical expenses.

Joan knows all the hard facts of a dancing career. But though she has no illusions about her future, this is still all she wants. And it is what most dancers want and continue to want until they either succeed or until their bodies rebel against the strict dance discipline, or unless they find themselves so badly in debt that they have to seek some other form of employment. Even dancers who work during the day in restaurants or at supermarket check-out counters attend class at night. Or they work at some job at night and go to class and to any audition that's open to them during the day.

Most, like Joan, went to their first ballet when they were five or six years old and fell hopelessly in love with what they saw on the stage. They, like Joan, have long since lost their illusions that ballet is a glamorous profession. They know that to be a dancer they must give up a great deal to gain a few moments of true exhilaration on the stage; that they will always be on a diet; that they will never be rich; and that they will work incredibly long hours for minimal pay; but they persist. That's really what dancing is all about. That, plus talent and an education that can cost up to seventy-five thousand dollars before a dancer is ready to perform.

As one mother, watching a son perform in the corps of a major ballet for the first time, said a little sadly: "For what it cost

to get John up on that stage, he could have been a brain surgeon
. . . well, I guess dancing is what he wanted. So that's what he
does."

If Joan is very good and very lucky, that's what she will do if
she passes the next audition, and if not that one, the one after
that.

4 Today's
Young Dancers

Four Young Ballet Dancers

How can anyone tell if a young teen-ager will make it as a dancer or not? That's a very difficult question. Of course, you have to have the right kind of body, you have to be musical and you have to have that special ingredient: talent. But a young would-be dancer's life is so different from that of a normal teen-ager's that there is one other quality that really counts: you have to want to dance more than anything in the world. When I talk to teen-agers, I give them one short test question: "Say the most attractive boy in your high school asks you out on a date. In order to go on that date, you have to miss class, would you go on the date?" If the answer is "yes" she probably won't be a dancer.

—HEATHER WATTS in an interview several years ago
when she was a member of
the New York City corps de ballet.
Today she is one of that company's eight
principal women dancers.

I T IS VERY EASY to think of dancers, particularly ballet dancers, as all being made of one piece. Their day-to-day lives, by the nature of their work, are very similar. Certainly, whether someone is a member of a company in London, Vienna, Moscow or New York, his or her schedule will look almost identical: classes, rehearsals, performances, dinner (usually light) and bed. And there will be the same activities at the same hours the next day, day after day, month after month, year after year.

Dancers in the New York City Ballet are similar in outlook as well as in schedules. They know that they are working for one of the greatest, perhaps *the* greatest, choreographers and ballet masters of all time. They also know that their future in their profession depends on whether and how they are noticed by Balanchine. In some ways, they worship him. In others, they fear him. In all ways, they want to please him, and they vie for his attention. They cannot do this in an obvious manner. From what everyone says about him, Balanchine is unmoved by flattery, detests dishonesty, considers that one's best efforts are simply a matter of course, and can spot talent (or the lack of it) and dedication (or the lack of it) from a distance of 100 feet. He dislikes sloppiness in dance, in appearance and in thinking. Balanchine is sometimes suspected by his dancers of having eyes in the back of his head. At any rate, he seems to be able to see a false move when, apparently, he is not even looking in the direction of the dancer.

To many casual onlookers, there often seems to be very little difference between one young woman in the corps and another, one young man jumping with almost incredible ease across the stage and another. In fact, some who are not very well informed criticize New York City Ballet dancers by saying: "They are all alike." Of course, they are not. They have their own personalities, ideas and hopes and fears. Dancing is, after all, a profession, and members of any profession have similarities in training, lifestyle and the importance they place on whatever it is they do best. Not all writers think alike, nor all physicians (including those in the same specialty and hospital), nor all lawyers or supermarket managers.

Being looked upon as carbon copies of each other is one of the aspects of their profession that bothers dancers most. "People think we live in special dancers' houses, eat special dancers' food, move around in special dancers' buses and feel special dancers' feelings," says Joseph Duell. "Nothing could be further from the truth. We are persons first . . . we are friends and brothers and sisters and sons and daughters, and we are more like other people our age than we are different. We are *ourselves,* and part of ourselves is the fact that we are also dancers."

Let us look at four dancers to see how they are different from young people in other professions, how they are like them, and most of all, how they are individuals who could never be mistaken for anyone but themselves.

Joseph Duell, Lourdes Lopez, Maria Calegari and Peter Frame have one important thing in common. They have passed all the early hurdles and are members of the New York City Ballet. This means that they can count on steady employment for much of the year. They go to company class, which means that they no longer have to pay for lessons, unless they want to study with an outside teacher as well. If they are sick or have sustained an injury that will keep them from dancing for only a week or so, they continue to receive a salary. And all four suspect from the roles they have been assigned within the past twelve months that they are on their way up.

A few years ago, all four were corps members. Lourdes was often the third swan from the left in the back row in George Balanchine's *Swan Lake.* Maria was often the third swan from the right. Balanchine likes to balance dancers. He may take brothers and sisters who resemble each other into the company, and then use them so that their look-alike qualities produce a special effect. He will sometimes also use two dancers who look as different from each other as possible as a balance to produce another kind of effect.

Lourdes and Maria belong to the second category. They are both tall, slender and beautiful. But otherwise, everything about them is different. Lourdes has long, straight, jet black hair, black eyes, and besides looking graceful, also appears strong. Her shoulders are a little wider than most women dancers', her legs look sturdy. Maria is a light strawberry blonde with a deceptive air of fragility about her. Their personalities are different too. Lourdes is very open, finds talking easy, and is warm and outgoing. Her special qualities of personality have made her a favorite with such diverse ballet personnel as the ushers who worry when she, for whatever reason, does not dance in a scheduled appearance; the secretaries in the offices, who sometimes stand backstage to watch her dance a newly assigned role; and even the people in the costume department, who don't mind refitting someone else's costume to her somewhat different proportions.

Maria is shy, finds it harder to talk, seems somehow emotionally, as well as physically, more fragile. She too has her fans among the staff members of the company; but, in her case, their admiration is most often expressed in terms of dancing, rather than personality. Few people know her well. When she is with her good friend Joseph Duell, he almost automatically does most of the talking. Maria listens.

Joseph Duell is one of the two brother teams in the company. Even for a dancer he is exceedingly good-looking. His most conspicuous quality, as a person, is his intelligence. He has had little formal schooling beyond high school except as a dancer, but he seems to be able to discuss music, art and other dance-related subjects easily. He seems organized; he knows exactly what he wants to do with his life now and twenty years from now. At first glance, Joe seems more secure than many of his fellow dancers.

Peter Frame has the body of a high school athlete and the face of a model for ski clothes. He is tall, taller than most of the other men in the company, blond and blue-eyed. He laughs a lot, and kids a lot. He, too, is part of a two-brother team. In his case the match-up technique of the choreographers works especially well. His brother Paul is his identical twin . . . and even those who know the two young men well often find it difficult to tell them apart. One way to tell the difference, for those who watch this company carefully, is to look at the casting. Who is dancing what? Peter, who came to ballet a few years earlier than his brother, gets major solo roles. In 1982, at any rate, Paul was often still a somewhat anonymous part of the thirty-member male corps de ballet.

Within four years, since they were first picked to be interviewed for this book, Lourdes, Maria, Joe and Peter have made enormous strides in their profession. Lourdes, Maria and Joe have been promoted to the fourteen-member-group of dancers called, at the New York City Ballet, "soloists." That is the rank between "corps" and "principal dancer." The distance between the corps and soloist is vast, much wider than the difference between soloist and principal. Soloists don't dance corps roles anymore. Each is assigned some principal roles in each season. All get a higher salary. They also get a dressing room with a name plate on the door, although most of them share the room with one or two other soloists. Most importantly, they have been recognized as being, in some way, special, as having qualities that in a no-star company like the New York City Ballet, makes them at least minor stars.

Joe has received even more special attention. For several years he has been chosen to choreograph pieces for the student production at the School of American Ballet, which is a learning and testing ground for would-be choreographers as well as would-be dancers. In 1982, he was asked to do one ballet for the company itself during the Tschaikovsky Festival. The piece was performed several times during the spring season, but will apparently not become part of the regular repertory. Yet for someone as young as Joe to have a work commissioned was an almost unprecedented honor.

Peter Frame is still nominally a corps member, but he has made a special place for himself in the company. Not only has he danced important solo roles, he has had several pieces choreographed for him. Unlike his three colleagues, he still occasionally appears as the third boy on the right or the fifth boy on the left in numbers in which the entire company dances. But more often he is assigned a special variation, a part of a dance in which he is alone on the stage. In the winter of 1982, he suffered a severe injury to his foot and spent the first months of the company's New York season at home in West Virginia. But other dancers have been injured much more severely and have come back within months. Often, after an initial setback, progress is even faster than it might have been without the injury. Perhaps those who decide on a dancer's progress in the company realize how much a good young dancer is missed when, for a time, he or she cannot perform.

Selecting dancers who may one day qualify as soloists when they are still corps beginners, when they are the fourth girl from the left, or the third boy from the right in any given ballet, is a favorite sport among balletomanes. Sometimes the dancers we pick fall by the wayside. They may be injured and have to stop

dancing. Or, occasionally, they may find a dancer's life too difficult and decide on some other company or profession. Lourdes,
Maria, Joe and Peter, however, are winners. They have more than
justified their early promise. All four are dancers about whom we
will be hearing a great deal in the years to come, barring, of
course, unforeseeable problems and injuries that can beset even
the most gifted and dedicated dancers.

Joseph Duell

I never wanted to be anything else. I really don't care what happens to me when I'm through. There is a certain amount of anxiety, which is constant, and which is part of all our lives. We strive for perfection . . . that's part of dancing. But there is also this tremendous amount of joy . . .

—JOSEPH DUELL in an interview.

WHEN HE WAS FIVE, he jumped over kitchen stools. When he was seven he started ballet classes. When he was sixteen, he came to New York from his home in Dayton, Ohio, to share an apartment with an older brother who was already in the New York City Ballet. From the day he started classes at the School of American Ballet, on a scholarship, he knew he was a dancer—for life.

Joseph Duell is one of five children. His father is an engineer who has always been interested in the arts. His three sisters took ballet classes at the Schwartz Sisters' School of Dance in Dayton for the reasons that so many young girls start dancing: their mother felt it would be good for their health and their postures. None of them gave a serious thought to dancing professionally, although one eventually majored in music at college.

When a male teacher joined the Dayton ballet school, Joe's father took him and his older brother to class there. The school was offering scholarships for boys because, although there always were plenty of girls who wanted to dance (mostly for the same reasons as the Duell sisters), there were very few boys. In Dayton, as in most towns in the United States, boys went to Little League; girls took ballet.

Dan, the older brother, was spotted by a talent scout for the School of American Ballet early on. He went to New York, lived in a house owned by dancer Jacques d'Amboise, who, with his wife, somehow managed to board and look after several would-be dancers a year, along with his own four children. By the time Joe came to New York to follow the same path as his brother (a scholarship at the School of American Ballet, and a job in the corps of the New York City Ballet Company), Dan was already a principal dancer with that company. That meant he could afford his own apartment. Joe moved in.

No matter how close a family is, competing with a brother who has already reached considerable heights in the profession one has chosen cannot be easy. Dan Duell was dancing most of the top male roles with the company; Joe was somewhere in the back, part of an anonymous group of male corps dancers. He tried hard to be noticed, perhaps at times a little too hard. He is a proud young man, on the surface at least, with almost unlimited self-confidence. Underneath there had to be self-doubts. Ballet, with its impossible goal of perfection, would give such doubts to any intelligent and sensitive person. And Joe has more of these qualities than most young men his age, although they are often hidden under a seemingly casual and carefree manner.

In his case, those doubts broke through after he had been with the company for several seasons and, in his opinion, was not getting much notice or attention. Dancing for him never seemed as easy as it did to his brother. The two young men look alike, but move very differently. Dan is fast and can perform spectacular jumps with apparent ease. Joe is elegant, lyrical, a wonderful partner. In short, as a dancer he has qualities that are not immediately apparent unless one watches him carefully over a period of time.

So, after spending one particularly frustrated and unhappy season, he went to George Balanchine and asked for a leave of absence. "I wanted time to think," he said, "to find a way to direct my life," He needed to take charge of his own future, unhampered by the constant reminder of his successful brother and the intense competition that, as a matter of course, exists in a company like the New York City Ballet.

According to Joe, Balanchine was both sympathetic and helpful. First, he suggested that he move out of Dan's apartment. Joe agreed and moved. For a while he worked as a sort of handyman —general house helper in the home of a New York family. It never occurred to him to quit dancing altogether, he says. Nor did he wish to change directions: try Broadway or Hollywood, for instance. He also did not wish to join another ballet company. That, in the end, really left no alternative: he came back to the New York City Ballet, this time with a firm knowledge that he was there to stay. If he could make it to the top ranks, fine. If not, he would still dance the Balanchine and Robbins choreographies he loved, even as a member of the corps. He had listened to a lot of music during the months he did not dance and was beginning to think that one of these days he might attempt to choreograph.

At first, there was little time for such plans. He had to get back into top dancing shape with endless classes, rehearsals, and, after only a month or so, performances, sometimes twice a day.

But leaving and coming back had removed many of his doubts about himself as a dancer and as a person. He stopped being in quite so much of a hurry. Because he was more relaxed and secure, the qualities that had always made him outstanding, his quiet elegance, his musicality, his ability to sense almost immediately what a choreographer wanted a series of steps to look like, came through. He was picked for a spot in a new and fiendishly difficult Balanchine choreography, *Kammermusik*, to a score by the modern composer Hindemith. He was still in the background, one of several dancers doing the same steps, but the corps in this choreography was small, and each of the young men chosen to dance in it had to have special talents.

That was the beginning. From then on, he was selected for ever more important solo roles. While still in the corps, he replaced another dancer as one of the principals in the Balanchine choreography, Bizet's *Symphony in C*, a piece that has become one of the signature ballets for the company. Dancers know that any new performer in one of those roles will at least receive critical attention from New York Ballet reviewers, if not necessarily praise.

Joe's performance got an enthusiastic headline in *The New York Time*'s ballet review the next day. The only trouble was that the headline writer got him mixed up with his brother, Dan. By now, Joe was able to laugh about the mistake, which might have hurt him deeply only a year before. The *Times* printed a little box the next day apologizing for the error.

Then he was picked to do a choreography for the annual graduation show of the School of American Ballet. Doing dances for a school performance may not seem like a major triumph to those who don't know New York's dance establishment. But being asked to do even a short piece for that school's production by Balanchine was a clear signal that, if he proved himself, his future in the company could be very bright indeed.

During the following two seasons, his brother Dan could not dance. He had injured his back, spent over a month in traction and had to come back slowly in special roles that did not require lifting dancers or catching them in midair. Dan had married one of the principal dancers in the company, Kyra Nichols, and Joe, partly because he looked quite a lot like Dan, found himself dancing his brother's roles, often with his brother's wife as a partner. Both brothers were pleased when Dan was able to come back to a full time schedule in 1981, and another source of potential tension and rivalry was eliminated. By then, Joe had his own roles in which he was firmly established and had been promoted to soloist.

Again, he was asked to do a choreography for the annual American School performance; this time to a longer piece with a difficult percussive score by modern French composer Darius Milhaud. The piece was called *La Création du Monde* (*The Creation of the World*) and, although it was jazzy and pulsating, the title suggested something of a story ballet: the rise of Adam and Eve from the early beginnings of life on earth.

Story ballets are not a large part of New York City Ballet Company's repertory, and a story of the world's creation was probably not what Balanchine had in mind when he assigned that particular score to Joe. At any rate, the approach did not work. Joe had to start over, and eventually created a piece that emphasized the rhythmic qualities of the score with a lyrical interlude for a male and female dancer at its center.

He considered himself lucky because he was provided with money to have special costumes designed and made for his twenty-eight dancers. Funds for the regular company for costumes and scenery are not noticeably generous; everything is used as often as possible, so one frequently sees a new or revived ballet with costumes that were worn by the dancers last year in another piece. Certainly the school performances generally feature costumes that have either been discarded or sidelined for several seasons by the parent company. So, with new costumes and a very different kind of choreography than he had first considered, Joe saw his piece at dress rehearsal. He was bitterly disappointed. It simply did not look the way he had imagined it.

Again, Balanchine came to the rescue. The costumes, he said, were terrible. And indeed they were. In order to suggest primitive fauna and flora, the dancers had been dressed in outfits that looked like body stockings with all sorts of ropes and fringes hanging from every part of their anatomies. The colors, browns, oranges, yellows and a particularly unattractive shade of green, tended to clash. All in all, what one saw was a very fine choreography, performed by excellent dancers, with everything being obscured by what Balanchine called "all that spaghetti."

Joe and the costume staff of the company and the school went to the storerooms and found simple body stockings in appropriate colors for the dancers. They scrapped the expensive special costumes, and the ballet emerged the way it had been originally designed: fast, exciting, with groups of dancers moving in imaginative patterns, and the two principals standing out from the crowd in a lovely, rather lyrical and romantic pas de deux.

Partly because of the success of that school performance, Joe, much to his surprise and joy, was assigned to do a choreography for the Tschaikovsky Festival scheduled for the New York City Ballet in the spring of 1981. He was by far the youngest choreographer so honored. His piece, a theme and fugue, used his ability to move groups of dancers in imaginative ways on the stage. Reviewers considered it "very promising" but, like many of the special pieces made by other choreographers for the festival, it was not taken into the permanent repertory of the company. Still, it was an outstanding beginning for a very young dancer who, only a few years ago, had been so beset by self-doubts that he had to stay away from dance altogether for a season. In 1982, he found, however, to his joy and surprise that *La Création du Monde* would be part of the NYCB regular spring season—minus the spaghetti costumes, of course.

What will happen to Joe in the years to come is, of course, difficult to predict. He says he doesn't think more than two years ahead, but, of course, he must, even though he may not realize that he is doing so. He talks of more choreographies, of roles sometimes created especially for him, usually together with Maria Calegari, who has become his most frequent partner. In any other profession, one would say that success had come early. After all, to be one of the most frequently seen dancers in one of the top companies in the world before one has even reached the age of twenty-five would be considered a success by most people. But Joe, like all other dancers, has one principal enemy: time. He has seen top dancers forced out of their careers because their bodies finally revolted against the stress and strain of ballet. By the time a male dancer is forty, his best years are almost always behind him. So Joe has another fifteen years to make it to the highest ranks of his profession. But he has many more years than that to become the kind of accomplished choreographer he could be. Combining dance with choreography is for dancers the best of two worlds. Joe just might make it in both.

Maria Calegari

Sometimes we have to learn three new choreographies in two weeks. We may not remember them in our heads . . . but our muscles remember.

—MARIA CALEGARI in an interview.

WHEN one looks at Maria Calegari, the last picture that comes into one's mind is muscles. She looks as if she spent her life in floating chiffon dresses: delicate, almost frail, with small bones, a heart-shaped face, wide-set eyes and long, full, red-blonde hair. At second glance, one realizes that she is quite tall and that her apparent fragility is an illusion. She does indeed spend a lot of her time in chiffon dresses; they happen to be a favored costume for the kinds of roles she is assigned. But that delicate fabric is as deceptive as the small bones. They hide a body that is totally disciplined, with each muscle trained to perform with perfect timing and balance.

By the end of the 1981 Tschaikovsky Festival, the New York City Ballet's ranks were sadly depleted by injuries. Among the principal female dancers, two had hurt their feet and were out of the company for the duration of the season, another was suffering recurrent back spasms. Maria took over many of the roles of these injured dancers, continued doing several that had been assigned to her from the beginning, and two that had been choreographed especially for her. During one weekend, toward the end of the season, she danced a principal role in every ballet that was performed, both during the matinees and the evening performances. She may look like everybody's image of a fairy princess, but, apparently, she has the kind of stamina any football player might envy.

Like most of the young woman in ballet, Maria started classes before she was ten. Unlike most of the other dancers, she is a native New Yorker, so that, while she was learning her craft at the School of American Ballet, she could live at home. She went from school directly into the company and spent the usual number of years as a corps member, dancing in a long row of swans, flowers, snowflakes, ballroom guests and other background figures.

There have always been many more gifted women in ballet, in general, and in New York City Ballet, in particular, than there have been men. With very rare exceptions, for a would-be ballerina, patience is an essential virtue—accompanied by hope. All of the young women in the corps (incidentally, they are always referred to as "girls," just as the men are called "boys," even when they reach, for dance, the ripe old age of forty) picture themselves as principal dancers eventually. For many, that hope has to be in vain. They remain in the corps; though, because the New York City Ballet encourages everyone with ambition and talent to learn principal roles, sometimes they get an unexpected chance to dance one of the roles they have studied.

Maria's career is not filled with sudden, unexpected leaps forward, just steady but sure progress. After a few seasons as the third girl from the right in the last row of the corps, she found herself in the front row. Because she is tall, she was cast occasionally with two or three other tall girls in ballets that required part of the corps to dance separately from the rest.

Suddenly, around 1979, she found her name on the casting lists for small solo roles. Dancers, including principal dancers, find out what they will be doing in a given week by looking at the casting call. Future roles are rarely discussed with dancers. The cast list, posted backstage, often as late as Sunday for the following week, is regarded with the same anticipation as grade averages in a particularly important and difficult high school or college course. The list can mean joyful surprise or deep disappointment.

Ballets are cast by whoever choreographed them; and at the New York City Ballet, more often than not, that means Balanchine. Indeed, one of the first indications that Balanchine has found a dancer interesting and talented may show up on that cast list.

From a corps swan, Maria moved to being one of the two solo swans. From one of two corps couples in the Tschaikovsky *Piano Concerto*, she moved to become one of the two women who dance in front of the company, one on each side of the principal dancer. (That meant she wore a dress of blue chiffon, instead of white.) Small solos became larger ones. With Joe Duell, she began to understudy roles in which the top dancers were cast regularly. And unlike Broadway understudies, who sometimes wait for years for a star to catch cold, ballet understudies almost invariably have a chance to perform. Even the strongest and healthiest principal occasionally succumbs to a strained muscle, a stubbed toe, an injured tendon. Dancers who are injured are not supposed to dance, and a principal who is secure in her art won't hesitate to allow an understudy to go on in her stead. Maria, in the course of a year, got to perform almost all the principal roles she had learned.

In the spring of 1981, she was promoted to soloist and was now permanently out of the standard corps roles. She also had the exciting experience of having choreographies created for her, both by Jerome Robbins and Joseph Duell, who made her the center of ballets for the company's Tschaikovsky Festival.

The Robbins role was accidental, in a way. The dance for a couple was supposed to be made for two stars of that no-star company, Peter Martins and Suzanne Farrell. But Martins was doing several choreographies of his own, and Farrell, besides being cast in many of the Tschaikovsky roles in the standard repertory, was having a special piece created for her by Balanchine. Between their other rehearsals, performances and choreographic sessions, Farrell and Martins never had time to learn the Robbins role: a lovely, lyrical, romantic dance to one of that composer's rarely heard piano pieces. Maria and Joe danced it at the gala opening of the Festival and throughout all of its performances from then on. They were still dancing it during the 1981–82 winter season. The reviewers loved them, and there was no reason to change a successful casting, although, originally, they had been considered understudies.

Maria is a serious dancer. Some of her admirers in the ballet audience wish she would smile more. When she is on stage, she look absorbed in what she is doing. When she takes her bows, she often looks as if she had not quite left the world of that last dance; as if the real world were something that she finds difficult to reenter.

She, like many of her young fellow dancers, simply has not thought about what she might do if and when she will no longer be dancing. It's a question almost every interviewer asks a young dancer . . . reluctantly, because for many dancers it is a question they would rather not hear and certainly not think about. "Maria is a very bright person," her friend Joe remarked when Maria just said that she could not imagine a life without ballet. "Maria could do anything she wanted to . . . and if she has to, she'll think of something else."

Of course, again barring injuries, Maria has many more years to be a dancer. She is already dancing many of the roles that are generally given to principals. What's more, she is now being cast in choreographies that are notably lacking in pale chiffon . . . the so-called "black and white" dances by Balanchine, often to the music of Stravinsky or Hindemith, in which the women wear skin-tight short black suits, sometimes with wide patent leather belts, showing every muscle in their bodies. She is no longer type-cast as a romantic ballerina, but is an all-around Balanchine dancer. At the moment, that is exactly what she wants to be. The chances are that Joe is right: eventually she will be able to do almost anything she wants to do, when she wants to do something other than just dance.

Lourdes Lopez

*I was flat-footed, pigeon-toed and had no calf muscles.
As a matter of fact, I was weak and wearing or-
thopedic shoes, and still kicking up a storm. So my
doctor said to my mother: "You know, she has to
develop some kind of strength, so why don't you en-
roll her in a ballet class?"*

— LOURDES LOPEZ in an interview.

THOSE BALLET CLASSES certainly must have done
wonders for Lourdes Lopez. To think of her today as a pigeon-
toed, flat-footed little girl requires a considerable leap of the
imagination. Today, Lourdes is one of the strongest, even sturdi-
est, of all the Balanchine dancers, for whom strength is a principal requirement.

She looks different from most of the rest of the company.
One critic compared her to a Renaissance portrait by a Spanish
painter. In the company of the rest of the New York City Ballet
women, she presents a contrast, dark rather than light, broad
shoulders rather than narrow. Her Cuban heritage shows, beautifully. At first glance she seems somehow mysterious. She could
play the part of the dark lady who seduces the innocent hero in a
spy picture. But, actually, she is one of the most open, easy-going
of the young dancers in the company. She is close to her family,
loves her work without apparently being deeply troubled by set-
backs, as many other dancers are, and has some decided and

realistic plans for a future, which she firmly expects to last beyond the age of forty, when her dancing days will most probably
be over. In fact, Lourdes, who is one of the most talented, hard-
working and dedicated young members of the New York City
Ballet, may also be the company's most realistic young woman.
She has come to terms with problems that almost all other
women dancers at the beginning of their careers prefer to ignore.
She knows she wants children, for instance, even though having
babies and ballet don't seem to mix very well, and she knows
that she may have to plan a whole second career sometime in the
as yet far-off and dim future.

She lives alone in a small apartment filled, not with autographed ballet pictures and discarded dancing slippers, but with
books. She reads a great deal, partly to make up for the formal
education she missed during the years she was training to be a
dancer, partly because she simply enjoys reading, and partly because of the realization that she will, eventually, be doing something other than dancing. She has even considered taking a few
college courses, specializing in child psychology. She considers
this field promising because she loves children and because, next
to being a dancer, the profession of child psychologist appeals to
her most. But she knows that for the time being taking full time
college courses is out of the question.

Because she is the kind of all-purpose dancer who can do
classical choreographies as well as modern ones, who looks
equally at home in dances by the three principal choreographers
in the company—Balanchine, Robbins and Martins—she travels
abroad a great deal. She has been on company tours to France,
England, Germany, Denmark and, most recently, China. She
reads guidebooks before every trip and asks others whom she
knows have traveled or lived in the countries she will visit what
museums she should see, what the important historical and ar-
chitectural monuments are, and where, if she has any free time
on the trip, she should spend it. Unfortunately, whether she is in
Paris, London or Peking, or at Lincoln Center in New York, free
time is seldom available.

Because Lourdes is hungry for experiences outside of dance,
she sometimes finds her trips frustrating. After all, when she is
in Paris, she would really like to go to the Louvre and see the
Mona Lisa. Instead, what she sees are her hotel room, the inside
of a taxicab, a backstage dressing room, class and rehearsal rooms

and the stage. All that changes for her, often, is the language spoken by the audience that comes to watch the company; otherwise, her dancer's life in Europe or Asia is only too similar to her life in the United States.

On her China trip she took advantage of every opportunity to learn as much about the country and its people as possible. The dancers were usually given two performance-free days to see the cities they visited: Peking, Shanghai and Canton. Lourdes spent the days she was not performing walking through museums, seeing historical monuments, shopping districts and anything else the company's English-speaking guide suggested. It was an exhausting, but also an exhilarating experience.

Everyone was expected to dance, and dance well, less than forty-eight hours after arrival. Jerome Robbins, who took the group of young New York City Ballet performers to China, can be a hard taskmaster. He expects perfection even after the dancers have spent more than twenty-four hours immobilized in uncomfortable plane seats. Apparently, they all managed to keep up with the schedule of performing plus sightseeing, although some, in talking about it, just sounded tired. Lourdes sounded enthusiastic. She would, however, like to return "as just a tourist" one of these days.

As a dancer, Lourdes had special qualities even when she first came to the company as a member of the corps. She radiates vitality. No matter how tired she is, a simple joy in dancing somehow comes through straight from her face and body, to the audience. It is interesting how different she looks from Maria Calegari, with her delicate, almost unearthly detachment. Both women do, at different times, the same solo dance in Balanchine's choreography to the *Tschaikovsky Piano Concerto.* Part of their variation involves a series of jumps (called *jetés* in ballet language) from the back of the stage through the corps, toward the audience. When Maria does this part, she looks as if she were, somehow, wafted up by an unseen force, a leaf floating upwards in a windstorm. She seems caught up in her own feelings, removed from all reality, including the audience that is watching her. There is no unseen force lifting Lourdes up from the floor of the stage. It is obvious that her own strong feet and legs are pushing her into those high jumps. Nor is she removed in any way from the audience. Her shining face, her flashing eyes and even her hands have a definite message: "Isn't this a wonderful ballet?" she seems to be saying, "and aren't I lucky to be dancing in it? And isn't it terrific that you are all out there watching it? All in all, isn't life just great?"

Yet, she was nervous when she first prepared for the role. "I had seen it danced by Kyra Nichols, who is one of the strongest technicians in the company . . . and I knew that, just from the technical point of view, that role can be exceedingly tough," she said. "I was a little scared when I first saw my name on the casting list. But I went out and bought the recording of the piano concerto and listened to it over and over again at home. The music is so marvelous, full of joy, as well as some sadness. My variation is mainly to the joyous parts. I also remembered what the costume looked like, a lovely blue with flashes of shiny stones like diamonds on the shoulders and at the waist. We wear rhinestones in our ears too. Then there is the scenery, tubes of clear plastic that, with the lighting used for this piece, make the stage look like a landscape filled with sun. I took the feelings that I experienced as I listened to the music with me on stage. 'If I am lucky, I'll get all the steps right, and I'll also be able to show how the piece affects me to the audience,' I thought. Once I was on, most of the nervousness went away. I was dancing, and, apparently, was able to master the difficulties reasonably well, but I was also continuing to feel what I had felt at home when I listened to the recording. I hope that this showed in my dancing." It did.

It is this quality of joy and enthusiasm, along with her superb technical strength, to which audiences respond.

There is one other skill she seems to show that many other Balanchine dancers don't have. Lourdes can act. In a ballet by Jerome Robbins, *Fancy Free,* Lourdes often dances one of the two girls who meet three sailors home on leave in front of a bar in New York City. The piece, choreographed almost forty years ago at the beginning of World War II, has the kind of innocence that no play or ballet on a similar theme would have today. The sailors pick up the girls, dance and flirt with them briefly, get into a fist fight over who will be the escort for which girl, and the girls walk out on the fracas. As the first girl the sailors meet, and whose red pocketbook they try to appropriate to keep her from leaving, Lourdes has exactly the right kind of flirtiness mixed with outrage, sympathy for the lonely guys mixed with a healthy instinct for self-protection that the part requires. One can understand exactly why the boys would be enchanted with her, why she would encourage them just a little, and then why she would leave when the situation threatened to become unpleasant. Lourdes, the dancer of 1980s, is perfect as this young woman from the 1940s. When she is dancing, the innocence, the slight sadness and the fun of the piece are evident to all.

Lourdes could have been almost anything she wanted to be: a child psychologist, a teacher, a wife and mother. She chose, without apparently any second thoughts, to become a dancer. As a dancer, she will perform at the top of her form as long as her body will let her. But of all the dancers we have met or will meet in this book, she may be the one who, eventually, can lead as happy and as full a life outside of ballet as she now does inside it. There are all those books she wants to read, all those museums she wants to visit, all that music she wants to hear, and all those children she wants to care for. And the fact that she apparently knows this about herself gives her a feeling of assurance and confidence that translates into a joyful, vital performance every time she steps on stage.

Peter Frame

Being in the corps in the company is different from being in the corps anywhere else. Almost all of our principals were in the corps once. Here, if you are good, you will probably be noticed and you will get roles of your own. That is what happened to Joe, Lourdes and Maria. I hope it will happen to me . . .

—PETER FRAME in an interview.

PETER FRAME looks unmistakably like a dancer, even from the back and with his foot in a cast. He walks like a dancer, with his hips and feet turned slightly out. He holds his head like a dancer—up. And when he hears music, even a snatch from someone's portable stereo or from a rehearsal piano in one of the studios at Lincoln Center, all of his muscles seem to jump to attention.

He has a perfect dancer's body: tall, slender, with a narrow waist and wide shoulders. He seems strong and graceful at the same time. Unlike many other dancers, he also has a very mobile face. Balanchine's dancers are rarely required to act. Even in the occasional story ballet that the company performs, action and feelings are shown mainly through body movements, not facial expressions. But Peter's face often mirrors the mood of the piece he is dancing. He can look serious, even a little fearful in something like the Robbins's *Dybbuk Variations*, a dance that hints at a ghostly presence that takes over the minds of the men who perform the piece. On the other hand, he can actually look as if he were having a ball in the ballroom scenes of a piece like Balanchine's *Vienna Waltzes.*

Of the four young dancers whose careers blossomed during the years this book was in preparation, he is the one who is still in the corps. But the roles he has been given have become increasingly more important. He—like Joe, Maria and Lourdes—often is asked to take the part of a soloist or even a principal. He was also one of the dancers Robbins took to China with him, and during the tour he got to dance roles he has not yet performed during the regular New York season.

His dancing days began, like Joe Duell's, because his sister was taking ballet lessons in their home town of Morgantown, West Virginia. He went to pick her up from a class, found that the school was also offering courses in gymnastics and decided that this was one way he could work off some of the excess energy that often seemed to get him into trouble.

The teacher, who, like all dance teachers, needed boys in his ballet class, offered him a scholarship. He took a few classes, mainly falling down and running into pillars, as he puts it. But he liked what he was doing and continued. With only a few weeks of dance training, he visited the North Carolina School of the Arts, where another sister was participating in a performance. One of the teachers there took one look at the tall boy who moved so gracefully and offered him a scholarship—without even an audition. He accepted and finished high school at the North Carolina institution where "they teach you every form of art known to man," as he puts it.

When he came to New York, he was accepted as an apprentice with the New York City Ballet, and, after a year, became a corps member. He has now been a regular part of the company for more than five years and has, like the other three dancers, not really considered any career except dance, although he knows how insecure the profession is.

After the China trip, when the company was still suffering from what one of the dancers called, "double jet lag," he danced with the New York City Ballet during a guest appearance in Boston. He had never been seriously injured, and at first felt more surprise than pain when the foot on which he put his weight during a fast turn suddenly seemed to collapse under him. He heard something snap, he says, but as so many dancers do when injured, he tried to stand up and continue as if nothing had happened. That turned out to be impossible. What every dancer dreads and tries not to think about had happened to him—he had been injured severely enough to be forced to leave the stage during a performance. Luckily, he was the last dancer in line, right near the stage wing. He somehow got himself off stage and collapsed on the floor. The physician who accompanies the New York City Ballet wherever it goes, and who is always backstage to make sure that an over-eager injured dancer does not go back on when injured, sent Peter to a hospital emergency room immediately.

An injury that might seem minor to almost any other young person can be crucial to a dancer. It could, if not properly treated quickly, permanently hamper a promising career, or even end it. Peter had broken a bone in his foot and, worse yet, had injured two tendons. This type of accident happens to many people, especially skiers. Usually their foot is put in a cast and they can go back to their regular jobs in less than a week. This, of course, is not true for a dancer. Peter knew immediately that it would be weeks and probably months before he could perform again. But he also knew that other dancers who had been injured much more seriously had come back and had managed to get themselves into better shape than ever before. In fact, during the Boston guest season, a principal dancer in the company, Robert Weiss, who had torn a vital tendon in his foot during a performance several seasons before, was back dancing for the first time in over a year.

After the Boston tour was over, Peter went home to West Virginia for a few weeks, but by Christmas time he was back in New York. Injured dancers, of course, cannot take class. They have to be sure not to do anything that will aggravate a potentially destructive physical condition. Since a working dancer's day is filled, from morning to late night, with classes, rehearsals, warm-ups and performances, day after day, month after month, year after year, many who cannot follow this highly structured and disciplined schedule don't know what to do with themselves if, for whatever reason, they are sidelined. Nondancing dancers have to look for new ways to occupy their time. They cannot even allow themselves to get depressed because most of the ways that the rest of us deal with depression make it harder for them to get back into shape once they start taking class again.

An injured dancer, for instance, cannot start eating bags full of cookies, or pints of chocolate ice cream, as many people do to cope with unhappiness. In fact, a dancer who cannot exercise must eat less than normal because putting on weight would cause additional problems. Most dancers don't drink alcoholic beverages, and many refuse to take painkilling or mood-altering drugs, because they feel, correctly, that the fewer chemicals they put into their bodies, the faster they will get back into dancing trim, once their injuries have healed.

Peter is clearly on his way up in a highly competitive company. His injury represented a temporary setback, but certainly not a change in career plans.

Because all dancers know what being injured is like (there is hardly anyone who has danced for longer than a few months who has not been hurt at least once), they are exceedingly supportive of a temporarily incapacitated colleague. The company works like a family . . . very competitive at times for the attention of the ballet masters, especially Balanchine, but also concerned, considerate and loving towards each other in times of trouble and crisis. Being part of a ballet company means that one must be able to trust one's fellow dancers. After all, even on stage, dancers must catch each other after jumps, support each other in arabesques and generally take care of each other. Trust is literally choreographed into their lives, and so is the need to work with other dancers and to help them when that becomes necessary. It is so much part of their art that, in many instances, it also becomes part of their lives.

By the 1982 spring season, Peter was dancing with the company again, and in several principal roles. He had already been signed up as one of the dancers who was going on tour in the Far East, to perform in Japan, Hong Kong and the Philippines during the NYCB summer break. Some of his friends hope that his injury has taught him one important lesson every dancer must learn early in life: if one is in too much of a hurry, one gets injured. Before his China trip, Peter had taken on free-lance assignments that had taken him to places as far removed from each other as Norway, Israel and Hawaii, all in less than six weeks. Just the travel alone must have been exhausting. It really would not have come as a surprise to a sports medicine expert that he hurt his foot the day he returned from China and tried to dance in Boston.

Peter also has a brother who is a physician, a sister who is an expert in emergency medicine and a mother who studied to be a nurse. With that much medical talent in the family, he will also probably receive a few stiff warnings from home.

Because of his natural endowments in appearance and talent, Peter can be expected to rise through the ranks. Like Joe, Maria and Lourdes, he may well become an important member of the dance world within the next few years. And he has one other advantage over most of his colleagues: he is still very young. For a dancer, the gift of time is worth more than almost every other gift. Peter still has all those extra years in which to dance, and almost everyone who has seen him feels that he has a long and very productive future before him. He still has not yet danced his greatest roles.

A Broadway Dancer: Susan Danielle

Prior to the first performance of A Chorus Line *at the Public Theater, the original company collectively appeared in seventy-two Broadway shows, with seventeen national companies, and on nine bus-and-truck tours in which they gave a total of 37,095 performances. Collectively they have had 612 years of dance training with 748 teachers . . . counting duplications. They spent approximately 894 dollars a month on dancing lessons. While performing they sustained thirty back, twenty-six knee and thirty-six ankle injuries. The characters portrayed in* A Chorus Line *are, for the most part, based upon the lives and experiences of Broadway dancers. This show is dedicated to anyone who has ever danced in a chorus or marched in step . . . anywhere.*

—Program note from the Playbill for *A Chorus Line.*

IF SUSAN DANIELLE were asked to describe her profession, she might well say: "I'm a gypsy." She doesn't read tea leaves, and her ancestry happens to be French and Irish. But, in show business language, a gypsy is a chorus dancer who goes from show to show, usually as a member of the corps, but sometimes also playing a featured part that requires singing and acting as well as dancing.

Danielle has worked in the Broadway hit show, *A Chorus Line*, for many months, and the song she sings has as its title, "Everything Was Beautiful at the Ballet." That's rather ironic, because Danielle started out to be a ballet dancer and hated every arabesque. Her mother ran a small dancing school in New Jersey, and she put Danielle in ballet slippers at the age of three. She took dancing lessons in her mother's school and later in New York City all through high school. Because she has the body and face of a classical dancer, her teachers kept encouraging her to continue. "You'll get to like this," they kept reassuring her. "Eventually, everybody who has the potential catches the ballet bug." Danielle didn't. One fine day she went home, hung her toe shoes in the closet and told her mother that as far as she was concerned ballet was for somebody else. She didn't like the highly structured movements, the music was too slow, and besides, the exercises hurt. "You really must enjoy pain to keep doing this all your life," she said. So, she decided to go to college.

Since she obviously had athletic talents, she chose physical education as her college major. During one summer she put her early dance training to good use by getting a job as a Rockette at the Radio City Music Hall. This gave her another chance to compare a career in dancing with one in education, and at that point, education still won out. Dancing as a Rockette for one summer was a lot of fun. She liked her fellow dancers and the many friendships she made at that time. "It was like belonging to a sorority," she said. "Some of the older women in the company loved the life at Radio City and the glamour of being known as a Rockette, so they stayed there for ten years or more. I thought it was great . . . for about four weeks. The dances were like military drills. We did the same steps over and over again. The only thing that changed were the costumes. By the time college started in the fall, I was so tired of kicking my legs in exact time and rhythm with a long line of other dancers that I really started to look forward to teaching gym."

But after she graduated from college and got her first practice teaching post, she found that physical education was not really her kind of career either. "Teaching gym was easier than dancing . . . and it certainly offered more security," she said. "But for me, it was just not challenging enough. The problem was similar, in a way, to being a Rockette. I could see myself doing the same things over and over again, year after year. I had the feeling that if I kept it up, I would wind up hanging in the equipment closet next to all those old sneakers."

She thinks that the day she told her mother she had decided to become a dancer may have been one of the happiest of her mom's life. But before anyone in the family could start looking for those discarded toe shoes, she made it clear that she still was not interested in becoming a ballerina. She had enjoyed the show business life at Radio City. If she could combine that lifestyle with a type of dancing that was not as structured as ballet and not as monotonous as the Rockette patterns, she felt she might finally have found the kind of work that would continue to interest and challenge her over the years. So, she began taking tap, jazz and modern dance.

Over the years she had looked carefully at many on-the-road musicals, and at the way films and TV used dancers. Dancing was changing, she noted, and the skills demanded from Broadway dancers were also changing. The long, uniform chorus line that had made the Rockettes a national institution was on its way out. Dancing in smaller groups, often with individual dancers doing special steps and routines was what the new choreographies were demanding. She also realized that those early ballet lessons had turned out to be an asset after all. Even after several years in which she had not danced, she was still in good shape, with strong muscles and flexible joints. Today she would advise any young man or woman who wished to become a professional dancer to take several years of ballet, even if that particular dance form was not his or her goal. "It gives you the basis on which every other dance form can be built," she maintains.

Because she had received good training, and because of her experience with the Rockettes, she got a job after her first audition, a rare occurrence. Many young dancers audition for months or even years, dance with small groups giving free performances in high schools and at social clubs, and work as waiters and salesclerks before they get their first professional job. Danielle was not yet in a Broadway show, but in one of the extravaganzas that dress designers, fabric houses and even automobile manufacturers put on annually in New York to introduce a new line to large groups of buyers. The shows are produced professionally, often with special music and choreographies, with good costumes, scenery and lighting, and always with professional performers.

Danielle's good luck continued. Right after the industrial show finished its week-long run, she attended an open audition for a major Broadway show. Often hundreds of would-be dancers show up at these auditions, during which usually no more than ten or twenty dancers are selected. But getting into one's first major show is important to any performer. To work on Broadway, in the movies or on TV, a dancer, a singer or an actor must belong to one of the performers' unions, (Actors' Equity for stage work, Screen Actors' Guild for movies and American Federation of Television and Radio Actors for television). To get an Equity card, one must be hired for an Equity show. And usually, in order to get into an Equity show, one must belong to the union. A nonunion performer who is picked for a union show must immediately obtain a union card, which marks the beginning of a serious career. Again, some performers spend years attempting to be hired for their first Equity production so that they can get that all important card. It's as vital to anyone interested in a career in show business as a license is to a physician or, for that matter, for a plumber or an electrician.

The fact that Broadway shows, motion pictures, TV productions and even commercials require that all performers be union members is, incidentally, one of the differences between these forms of entertainment and ballet companies. In most ballet companies, the musicians, the people who move the furniture, work on the lights, and make the costumes all must be union members. The dancers rarely belong to unions. Among the major companies, only the American Ballet Theater is now unionized.

Actor's Equity, (with other performers' unions) sets minimum wage standards and working conditions for its members. Featured players usually have agents who negotiate their clients' salaries separately (although in a Broadway show, everyone from the dancers in the last row of the chorus line to the major star with his name in lights *must* belong to Equity to work). The union makes sure that all chorus members get paid a living wage for rehearsals and performances and enough money to live on when the show is taken on the road . . . when the performer is working, of course.

Broadway performers, and especially gypsies, have an even more insecure professional life than ballet dancers who are steadily employed by one company. A chorus dancer will start with a show when it begins to rehearse. Salaries during rehearsals are lower than salaries during performances. And, of course, a Broadway show can close down after a few days if the reviews are poor or if, for some other reason, ticket sales are not enough to keep the backers from losing too much money. So, a gypsy can have spent a few weeks rehearsing at relatively low pay, hoping to make a good salary once the show opens, only to find that he or she is out of a job entirely with less than a week's wages. Unlike union members who work for manufacturing companies, for instance, Equity players don't get severance pay. Once the show closes, the paychecks stop. Of course, a TV show or a film has its own built-in termination point. When the production is completed, the dancers are out of a job, no matter how successful the show turns out to be.

Most Broadway gypsies hope that they will be hired for musicals that turn into hits, which may run for several years in New York and often even longer on the road. Even for those lucky ones, there is a problem: after doing the same dances and songs seven times each week (five evening performances and two matinees), almost anyone will get bored or stale in a role. Major stars know this and usually limit the time they commit themselves by contract to stay in one show, no matter how successful it may turn out to be. Most have a fair idea of their own tolerance for performing the same role over an extended period of time. When they feel that the performances are becoming a boring chore rather than an enjoyable experience, they leave that show and find a new part, either in another Broadway venture or in a film or TV show. They are then replaced by another well-known performer or, occasionally, by a lucky understudy (who might just be a gypsy . . . this is one way gypsies get ahead). But a gypsy who quits a show because he or she just cannot face another week or month or year of the same routine really does not have the same options as a star. There usually is not another show just waiting for him or her to step into. It may take weeks or months, or sometimes as long as a year, to line up a new assignment, and it is a brave gypsy who quits a show before having another job lined up.

Susan Danielle does not take daily class the way most dancers do. One of the reasons she does not is that she uses the time that class would take to go to auditions for other shows. She still enjoys her role in *A Chorus Line*, but she can see the day coming when singing about how wonderful everything is at the ballet, and doing her dance routine, may become as deadly as teaching gym or kicking her legs as a Rockette. She is constantly looking for other small jobs she can do while still in her present show. These days, TV commercials are using more and more dancers, and Danielle finds that she can make extra money doing commercials, as well as getting a break in her routine. But for every commercial she gets, she attends four or five auditions.

Actually Danielle has an interesting role in *A Chorus Line*: a somewhat over-age, cynical dancer called Sheila who manages to combine a dry sense of humor about her profession with a certain sense of sadness at the knowledge that her dancing days may soon be over.

A Chorus Line is a show that gives many unique opportunities to performers who formerly were just dancers. The story is a simple one: a director-choreographer is casting a show that will, in the end, be very much like *A Chorus Line*. In fact, it may even be *A Chorus Line*. An open call has been issued and almost 100 dancers have turned up to try out for the eight parts that will be available. They are allowed to show what they can do in large groups and, at every turn, many applicants are eliminated. Eventually about twice as many dancers as will be needed are asked to stay and are requested to tell the choreographer-director something about themselves. He hints that in the show he is producing he wants dancers who have special qualities that will make them stand out as individuals, rather than just as members of a group. Each dancer tells his or her story, some haltingly, some easily, some boastfully, and some very shyly.

As it turns out, very few of these dancers have had easy lives. They had not made the kind of progress in their careers they had hoped. Most have had serious problems in their personal relationships with parents, lovers and colleagues as well. Most keep hoping that life will get better (just as they hope to get a job in the show), but underneath all the talk, songs and dances, the audience is aware that only one or two of these performers will have a chance to lead a satisfactory professional or personal life.

Basically, *A Chorus Line* is a profoundly pessimistic musical. And the character Danielle has been playing is one of those who never had a chance in the first place. At thirty, she's already too old.

Does the real young dancer, Danielle, think that *A Chorus Line* is a realistic picture of her chosen profession? Yes, she does. Does she therefore fear that her career may go the way that Sheila's is going? No, she doesn't. Gypsies, by nature, almost have to be optimistic (a point that *A Chorus Line* makes), and Danielle actually has many more reasons for optimism than most of the characters in the musical.

In the first place, she has had an important early success. She probably will never have to go to an open chorus audition for a musical again. After all, she has already successfully played a featured role in a major Broadway hit. In the second place, she has found that she has a talent for singing and acting as well as dancing. She still takes an occasional dance class, but much of her extra time now goes for acting and singing lessons. As she puts it: "Singers and actors last a lot longer than dancers. They may get arthritis in their knees, but they don't lose their voices. And there are lots of roles for nice old ladies in many plays. There are many middle-aged actors around . . . but almost no middle-aged dancers." She is right, of course, and she is realistically getting ready for a future in which she may not be dancing at all but getting good acting and singing parts. She is making sure now that when she is actually as old as Sheila, the character she plays in the show, she will have all kinds of options open to her.

"Shirley McLaine was a gypsy twenty-five years ago," she says. "Look at her now. At her age, a ballerina would have long been at the end of her career. She might even be thinking of becoming a gym teacher. But Shirley has been doing some of her best work in the last two or three years. She still has years of stardom before her. I'm going to try to use her as a model. She's wonderful, and I admire her a lot. And then she also has all those options . . . I don't think teaching physical ed is one."

An All-Around Dancer: Ronald Brown

In Cleveland my grandmother danced tap. My mother was with a modern dance company. I never really thought of becoming a dancer. But one day I just found out that I was one.

—RONALD BROWN, in an interview.

ONALD BROWN is teaching a class at Alvin Ailey's American Dance Center School on Broadway near Schubert Alley. The school, which contains two floors of studios plus a few small offices and a tiny teachers' lounge, is jammed with people, most carrying dance bags flung over their shoulders. Those who know the Ailey company generally think of it as a black group. Actually it isn't. One of the principal women is white, several of the outstanding soloists are Japanese, and Ailey himself has often said that he looks for *good* dancers, who can perform in a variety of styles. But most of the company members are indeed black. The school, at least on that Saturday afternoon, however, was a truly integrated place. Not only were there black, white and Oriental students, but also students of all ages, from a three-year-old with pony tails whose mother was being told firmly that her daughter was still too young for advanced classes to the middle-aged homemaker who took tap to lose a few pounds, to the police officer who was taking jazz dancing because, he said, it relaxed him. Many of the students in the advanced classes were clearly either professionals already or on the way to becoming professionals. But in the beginning classes there were students taking their first dance steps . . . and some of them were over forty years old.

Brown teaches beginning ballet. There are about a dozen men and women in rehearsal clothes at the barre, ranging in age from about sixteen to about forty-five. A bored-looking pianist is playing a Chopin waltz. The room looks and smells like any dance studio, anywhere. One hopes, however, that nobody in that class has even the remotest intention of becoming a professional dancer. Everyone is having a fine time . . . but there is a good deal of huffing and puffing, with everyone trying, to the best of his or her ability, to do the simple warm-up routine that Brown is showing them. Does *anyone* in the class come because he or she has enough talent to make it in the highly competitive dance field? "Well, not really," says Brown. "But that guy over there has a good body and a fine sense of music. He's a bit old to be starting . . . but perhaps, if he keeps at it . . ." Brown goes over to the young man and shows him how to change the position of his leg. Then he comes back. "Well, it's a long shot at best," he admits.

Brown is teaching this morning because the Ailey Company, which has just completed a two-month New York season, is on a break. For him, it's either teaching or going on unemployment. And, of the two, Brown definitely prefers teaching.

"Actually, I find I get something out of these classes for adult beginners," he says. "Dancers are by nature terribly impatient people. We tend to be impatient with others . . . and most of all we tend to be impatient with ourselves. If our bodies don't want to do what we think they should be able to do we get angry. And then we tense up. And tense dancers get injured. I just got over a fairly serious hip injury myself. Teaching these students requires patience. You have to show each one of them over and over again how even the simplest step should look. And by learning to be patient with them, I have become much more patient with myself. I can tell myself now that even if I can't get those difficult air turns right on the first attempt, I'll simply have to try for the second or third time. Also, while watching newcomers to dance struggle with beginning routines, some of us realize that we have come quite a long way since *we* started dancing. We tend to forget that . . . we see so many wonderful dancers around us that we begin to believe dancing is like breathing. You must do it from instinct. Of course it's not instinct . . . it's years and years of practice. So, in a way, teaching beginners is good for me. I hope it's good for *them* too."

He looks at a teen-ager who is clearly taking dance to overcome a weight problem. "No, Joan," he says. "You turn on the left leg . . . look at yourself in the mirror." Joan turns on the right leg again. "You still don't seem to get the hang of this," he says. "Here, let's try to do this together." Like any good dancing partner, he puts his hand on her waist and helps her to turn . . . the right way this time. For a second plain, overweight Joan seems to feel like a ballerina. She looks at herself and Brown in the mirror and smiles. Then she does the turn by herself—correctly.

Brown is an Ailey dancer on the way up. He has come a long way since his childhood in Cleveland, when his third grade teacher, watching him in gym class, suggested that he apply for a scholarship at a dancing school called "The Ballet Russe of Cleveland." He had been dancing ever since he could remember. "I showed off at parties; I danced to bongo drums on the street; I think I felt like dancing whenever I heard music anywhere," he said.

All of his dancing classes have been on scholarship. After high school in Cleveland he came to New York to the Ailey school (the part that's for professionals, not the Saturday morning class for amateurs and beginners). He was accepted into the Ailey Two Company, a group of promising young dancers who spend time dancing in schools, colleges and church basements to get experience. After a year he was asked to join the corps of the senior company and has been dancing with that group for more than three years now. He has toured throughout the United States and Europe, and he is beginning to get important solo roles assigned to him.

"Next season we will have three new dances in the repertory. So far one piece has been cast. I'm in it. The other two are still in tryout," he says. Obviously he hopes to get a part in one or both of those new pieces as well.

Meanwhile he is taking daily company class and, in addition, some special classes in tap and jazz for which he pays. "Ballet is a good foundation for any kind of dancer," he says. "But it's still very difficult for a black man to make it in a ballet company. Until a few years ago it was almost impossible. Now, of course, some of the best companies are hiring black dancers. But it's still better if you can do many different kinds of dance. And besides, I enjoy performing in many styles and to all kinds of music."

Ailey dancers don't use the standard ballet steps and positions. The women do not wear toe shoes. Even one choreography that Ailey made for the American Ballet Theater (*The River,* to the music of Duke Ellington) is done by the Ailey woman dancers in flat dance shoes, not on point. Ailey's company has its own unique style, a combination of ethnic dance, jazz, tap, Broadway, with a slight overtone of classic ballet movement, especially for the men.

What Brown does as a dancer is neither easier nor more difficult than what Joe Duell and Peter Frame do at the New York City Ballet. It's just different.

The Ailey season is shorter than that of NYCB or American Ballet Theater. Company members spend some time each year either finding other dancing jobs (many do commercials) or teaching, or, when necessary, collecting unemployment. The life of an Ailey dancer is a kind of cross between that of a Broadway gypsy and a soloist in a major ballet group. Ailey dancers have to be available for the New York season and for company tours. They are expected to take company class every morning and to be available for rehearsals, even during the between-season weeks and months. So they cannot find jobs in Broadway shows or in Hollywood musicals. They have a little more security than the Broadway dancer who is between shows. They know that in a week or a month they will get that regular paycheck again. But they also do not have quite as much security as dancers with a company like the New York City Ballet, which is able to guarantee its members almost fifty weeks of steady employment a year.

So far, Brown has spent relatively little time on unemployment. "I sometimes get a short engagement away from New York," he says. "I have danced in Florida with a small company recently, for instance; but as far as I am concerned, the Ailey company is my career. I would not miss a performance even for a high-paying commercial. I probably wouldn't even miss a rehearsal or a class. I think I'm a good Ailey dancer. I hope Mr. Ailey agrees with me."

Watching Brown doing those three air turns he said he took him three rehearsal periods to perfect and realizing that, in his about twenty years of life he has already learned and danced over forty different choreographies, one would tend to think that Mr. Ailey probably does agree.

*Joe Duell, when he was still
a member of the corps,
in a Balanchine ballet.*

Maria Calegari and Joseph Duell
are often cast together.
Here they are
in Balanchine's "Emeralds."

Maria Calegari, now a soloist,
in "Emeralds."

*Lourdes Lopez
substituted for
an injured
principal dancer
in* The Four Seasons,
*a Robbins ballet.
She was so good
that she has been
dancing the role
ever since.*

*Lourdes Lopez,
partnered
by Peter Martins,
in one
of Balanchine's
so-called "black
and white ballets"
(women in black
tunics, men in
white T-shirts
and black tights).*

*Peter Frame,
looking terrified
in a ballet
about Dybbuks
(Jewish ghosts)
by Jerome Robbins.*

Ronald Brown,
a dancer in the Ailey company,
teaches a class on Saturdays
to help pay the rent.

Susan Danielle, a Broadway "gypsy,"
backstage at the long-running
hit show A Chorus Line.

5 The Super-dancers

CHAPTER XVII

What Makes
a Superdancer?

Stars don't depend on billing; sometimes they don't depend on ability, although this is far less true in dance than it is in the movies. Ballet stars happen through a combination of style, strength, technique and high concentration of energy; and when people see one they know he is there no matter what company policy may be.

—JOSEPH H. MAZO in *Dance Is a Contact Sport.*

HERBERT ROSS knows a star when he sees one, in the movies as well as in dancing. He started his professional life as a dancer and became a choreographer whose works are still performed by major companies throughout the world, although he has long since left ballet for motion pictures. He is a film director who manages to work on at least one major hit movie each year. He is married to a former ballet star, Nora Kaye, perhaps the first American-born, American-trained ballerina to achieve international fame and to have several major choreographies made for her. Today, she is Associate Director of the American Ballet Theater, whose principal dancer she once was. She also works as producer for many of the movies her husband directs.

In two instances, at least, she was the driving force behind the films: *The Turning Point*, which introduced Mikhail Baryshnikov to a whole new generation of potential balletomanes, and *Nijinsky*, a biography of that dancer, which intrigued many dance lovers but left some critics and most of the public quite cool.

The Turning Point, which dealt with the rivalry between two women who had been friends in their early years, won several Academy Awards, including one for Baryshnikov as the best supporting actor (he spoke very little English at the time the film was made), and was also a huge box office success. *Nijinsky*, which dealt with the relationship between the dancer and the impressario, Diaghilev, reproduced in fascinating detail the ballet world of fifty years ago. It was not a box office success. Somehow, the real Nijinsky was of less interest to the public than the fictional characters who populated *The Turning Point*.

What makes a technically great dancer also a star? What made Nijinsky a star in his day? Ross feels that he or she has to have some special quality that impresses the public sufficiently to make the dancer remembered even when his or her dancing days are over. There may be roles associated especially with that dancer that no later performer, no matter how competent, has ever been able to dance in quite the same convincing way. The dancer may have possessed personal fascination, along with an individual style that belonged to him or her alone.

Anna Pavlova and Vaslav Nijinsky were such superdancers. They are remembered because of what was said and written about them in their own time. Most of the pictures we have of these dancers are posed photographs. When attempts were made to take pictures of them during a performance, the result was mainly a blur. But there was an aura about them that survived.

Dancers, in those days, were known to a select few. They were not celebrities the way actors and actresses, political figures or sports figures were. This is still true today. With the possible exception of Baryshnikov, today's star dancers are not generally celebrities whose every move is followed by gossip reporters and tabloid newspapers. They are thought of as artists, as well as entertainers, and, in that way, the impression they leave on the public's mind is more like the image of a classical musician, a painter or a serious writer.

In some ways, this is an advantage. Dancers like Peter Martins, Jacques d'Amboise, Suzanne Farrell, Patricia McBride, Cynthia Gregory and Natalia Makarova can walk down a street or eat in a restaurant almost anywhere without being mobbed by adoring, but bad-mannered fans. The people who admire them tend to do so at a respectful distance. Even Baryshnikov can give an interview, sitting at a picnic table on the grounds of the Saratoga Arts Festival, without being surrounded by a mob. People who know who he is (and most who are on the festival grounds have seen him dance) may stop to look at him. But if he waves someone away, or says quietly, "I can't autograph now . . . I am giving an interview," they will leave without showing anger or resentment, as they might if he were a popular rock star, for instance.

Occasionally, of course, there are dance fans with bad manners. Just like the ordinary variety of autograph hunters, they will approach a dancer eating lunch or walking along a street with an urgent request for an autograph. But such incidents tend to surprise dancers, where they would be taken as a matter of course by any motion picture or television personality, who expects to have little privacy when they appear in public. When a dancer's privacy is invaded, he or she tends to look more amazed than annoyed.

It is often surprising how much a serious dance fan knows about the *professional* life of a favorite dancer and how little concern is shown for that dancer's private life. Balletomanes tend to read dance reviews, not gossip columns. They seem to believe that the only duty a dancer has to his or her public is to give the best possible performance. Dancers, unlike rock stars and movie actors, have not become public property. Their fans don't feel as if they own them, or as if they somehow created them, and therefore, they owe it to the public to sacrifice their privacy and dignity. The public did not create dance stars; they created themselves.

Herbert Ross, partly from the reaction he has received to his ballet movies and partly from his wife's experiences at the American Ballet Theater, feels that some young Americans have given top dancers a sort of hero status, and that this type of adulation is different from the kind of curiosity and fan club admiration accorded current popular celebrities. In his opinion, what young people admire about dancers is their discipline and their obvious dedication to their work. "There are so few fields in which discipline is still required," he says. "In fact, in the past decade or so, discipline sometimes seems to have gotten a bad name. But many of these youngsters are looking for a serious direction in their own lives. They respect the results of this discipline, if not the idea of it. And in dance they can see the results. When they watch someone like Baryshnikov dance, they know that *nobody* could do what he does without putting in years of unremitting hard work. Dancing, to be really good, has to look easy, perhaps sometimes even casual, but underneath the apparent ease of great dancing, there is something that reflects the hard work that goes into this art form. So dance in general and ballet in particular may be reaching and moving more young people today because it is an island of dedication and serious effort in a slipshod world."

But there is another reason why dance is achieving increasing popularity with the young; this art form is no longer relegated to the status of a museum piece. Dancers now appear in high school and college auditoriums; dance is accessible to all on television. "We have tried to demystify the world of the dancer, to show dancers as people, and ballet as something that can be enjoyed, rather than studied in a classroom," Ross says.

Dancing is an art form, certainly. But it is also fun and entertainment. At its best, dancing has to be technically and artistically valid. Yet Baryshnikov and Balanchine have both said that the dancers they admire most are Fred Astaire and James Cagney. When these men were doing their Hollywood musicals, nobody considered these films "art."

Art, then and now, tends to be looked upon like health food: something that is certainly good for you, that your mother and aunt would approve of, but that's also vaguely boring and out of date. For decades dance, except as seen in the movies, and especially ballet, was filed away by most young Americans as an uplifting but not very entertaining experience. As dance has become more accessible, more people have come to look on it as part of their lives.

It's interesting to note that while, in the nineteen-thirties, forties and even still in the fifties, most of the superdancers appeared in movies or on Broadway, today they are almost entirely in ballet. Baryshnikov may appear on film or on TV, but he is still always a ballet dancer, unlike the stars of past decades: Fred Astaire, Ginger Rogers and Bill Robinson for instance. The reason for this is that Broadway and film choreographers are using dance in an entirely new way, which makes the choreography, rather than the individual dancer, the star.

Agnes de Mille and Jerome Robbins used dance in Broadway musicals as an integral part of the plot. Directors and choreographers like Herbert Ross and Bob Fosse often use dance the way the ancient Greeks used their chorus: as a commentary on the action and as an expression of the philosophy behind the story. This technique works best when attention is focused on a group of dancers rather than on an individual.

For instance, in Fosse's *All That Jazz,* dances are used to mirror part of the principal character's life, to comment on it and to judge it. In one sequence the main character—who has undermined his health and all of his relationships through excesses in drinking, smoking, drugs and sex—undergoes open heart surgery. Graphic operating room scenes are alternated through very clever cutting and editing with dances that show the shallowness, the insecurity, the inability to love and the self-destructiveness of the character who, incidentally, is a motion picture director and choreographer, very much like the man who made the film. Fosse has said in interviews that some of the film is autobiographical. He, himself, had open heart surgery, and he made the movie almost immediately after he recovered his health. In the film, the character does not recover (and thus, presumably, gain another chance to become a better person). He dies. *All That Jazz* makes its whole point through dancing. Without the dance sequences, the movie could not have existed as a statement of the meaning of life and death.

Pennies From Heaven, produced by Herbert Ross and Nora Kaye (who, as mentioned earlier, both started their professional careers as dancers), is a film about illusion and reality. The reality is the despair and poverty of the Great Depression in the early 1930s. The illusion is the never-fading hope of some of the characters that somehow, some way, everything will turn out just fine. The reality is acted. The illusions are danced in production numbers that look a lot like the movies that were actually made during the early thirties, with high-stepping chorus girls kicking their legs on moving platforms or tapping down a long flight of stairs. There is one scene in which dozens of little girls and boys dance, in glittering evening clothes, on shiny white pianos. The children of both sexes manage somehow to resemble the young Shirley Temple, whose early movies were designed specifically to make our parents and grandparents forget the misery of the Depression years.

The reality behind the dance scene is a schoolroom, filled with restless, shabby youngsters. The dance comes to a sudden end when the school principal enters the room and cruelly punishes a harmless little boy by striking him over his knuckles sharply with a ruler. The boy, typically, looks especially trusting and friendly, but he is also overweight and clumsy. His trust is an illusion: he is the butt of everyone's frustration.

Ross uses those dances to take us back to a time when people comforted themselves by believing that what they saw and experienced was not the truth. They chose to live in an illusion and to believe that the words of the popular songs of those days were somehow more real than the life they led: that someday pennies would indeed come raining down from heaven; that life was just a bowl of cherries; and that there was gold on the other side of the rainbow. As we see more of these kinds of illusion, expressed by dance, we realize suddenly that Ross is not talking about the 1930s at all. He is talking about *right now*. What he is saying is shown in the contrast between the song-and-dance numbers and the actions of his characters: that illusions may keep us temporarily from being too miserable, but in the end, we have to deal with reality and make it more bearable if we and our world are to survive. If all of that had been said in words, the motion picture would have been preachy, dull and not very original. But it is all said with dance—and the point is made both subtly and brilliantly.

But this type of choreography does not produce dancing stars. Indeed in some of the best choreographies nondancers are given principal dancing roles: Steve Martin, Bernadette Peters and Christopher Walken in *Pennies From Heaven*, for instance.

Today's superdancers are in ballet because of the nature of that particular art. Because, as ballet dancers, they now appear in movies and on television where millions rather than thousands are able to see them perform, we are producing a whole new generation of balletomanes, and some of these ballet fans have never seen a superdancer in person. They have learned the magic that these artists produce by sitting in the local movie house or watching the TV screen. Even the best-filmed performance can never be quite like watching live dancers on stage, but film does make their art accessible to young people who might never have been exposed to the best of ballet in the not-so-distant past.

CHAPTER XVIII

Baryshnikov

For some of us, ballet is not a profession, it is a religion.

—MIKHAIL BARYSHNIKOV

THE PIANIST paused for a second as he moved from one passage to the next in a Chopin nocturne. As the music briefly faded, a dancer, dressed in brown tights and a white shirt, bent his knees slowly and gently touched the floor with his palm. With that gesture, the stage floor suddenly became the warm earth, smelling faintly of early fall. As the music rose, so did the dancer. He looked towards the ceiling, and that ceiling became an autumn sky with moonlight fading into early morning darkness. The audience at the New York State Theater was completely still, every eye focused on the young man who had the body of a seventeen-year-old high school gymnast and the somehow ageless face of a poet or mime. Mikhail Baryshnikov was doing what he does best: mesmerizing an audience and creating, with no props but the music and the movement of his body, a moment of total illusion.

That evening he was dancing the Boy in Brown in *Dances at a Gathering*, a plotless ballet created more than ten years before by choreographer Jerome Robbins for a group of young soloists at the New York City Ballet. The most surprising fact about Baryshnikov's performance was not its brilliance, or even its power to move an audience to tears, but the fact he was able to dance the role at all, and that he could adapt to a new way of life, of dancing and of relating to a company when all of his early training had pointed him in a completely different direction.

Then he was thirty-one years old and had been in this country for less than five years. Today, four years later, he is the artistic director of yet another large, internationally known ballet company, the American Ballet Theater. He still dances, but he is called upon to be an organizer, a planner and a director, all roles for which his training did not prepare him at all and which he seems to fulfill with almost as much ability as he showed when dancing.

At thirty-five, he seems to have lived through several different lives. At twenty-five, he was a ballet idol in the Soviet Union, the youngest dancer ever to win its State Award of Merit. He left the Kirov company, and his native land, and joined the American Ballet Theater, where he immediately became a star. His far-famed jumps and twirls in the classical story ballets brought instant praise. The mention of his name with any dance performance immediately sold out the house. He made his motion picture debut in *The Turning Point* and won an Academy Award nomination for his role, although at the time the film was made, he spoke very little English. His picture appeared on the covers of *Time* and *Newsweek*, and almost every move he made was covered by a spate of gossip columnists and paparazzi.

Almost overnight, Baryshnikov had become an international superstar, complete with hysterical groupies who seemed to range in age from eight to eighty. But the role of superstar made him distinctly uncomfortable. He seems most comfortable with other dancers, small children and animals.

Baryshnikov *is* a very private person. He gives very few interviews. When he does, he talks about what he calls "my job," which happens to be dancing. He considers his personal life, present, past and future, no one's business but his own. A reporter who asks what he considers an unsuitable question gets a short: "I don't want to talk about that." He will discuss eagerly and enthusiastically ballets he has seen, artists he admires most: Fred Astaire, Charlie Chaplin, whom he resembles, and George Balanchine. But a reporter who asks a personal or otherwise indiscreet question will find that the expressive face has turned stony and cold.

Because so little is really known about Baryshnikov, most of his fans have the impression that he actually *is* the dancer he played in *The Turning Point:* a rather feckless, thoughtless young man who happens to dance exceedingly well, but who spends most of his time chasing beautiful budding young ballerinas. As it turns out, the character he played and the actual man have very little in common except that they inhabit the same body, can perform spectacular acrobatic feats on the ballet stage and speak with a Russian accent. Baryshnikov is a serious artist to whom work has always come first. He made that very clear when he announced to a shocked dance world that he was leaving the safe haven of the American Ballet Theater, where he was the undisputed top attraction, to join the New York City Ballet, where he would be just one more male dancer. If there was a way to resign voluntarily from superstardom, Baryshnikov apparently found it.

The New York City Ballet has two New York seasons, a Washington, D.C. season, a Saratoga Arts Festival season, plus in recent years, a summer foreign tour. All dancers, from corps members to top principal dancers, are expected to be available for all performances during these periods unless they are injured or sick. They dance up to six times a week, a schedule that makes dancers in other companies shudder. In some ballets a principal dancer may be assigned a minor role while a talented corps member dances a major one.

To join the New York City Ballet, Baryshnikov gave up about two-thirds of his income. All principal dancers in that company are paid about the same salaries, modest compared to what the American Ballet Theater offers its stars. But Baryshnikov sacrificed a great deal more than money. He lost much of his personal freedom. He committed himself to a schedule that few other dancers have ever attempted. Most dancers learn two or three new ballets a season. Baryshnikov learned about twenty in his first year with the New York City Ballet. What's more, he had to adapt to an entirely different repertory and a style of dancing that was new to him. The plotless choreographies of Balanchine and Robbins concentrate on pure movement, and most dancers not trained by Balanchine find them fiendishly hard to learn and tricky to perform. Almost all the principal dancers in the company are graduates of Balanchine's school. The few male dancers who were trained in Europe joined the company in their early twenties, or even earlier, and spent a decade perfecting their techniques. Baryshnikov was already thirty when he joined, and the professional life of a male dancer tends to peak at about that time. So the decision to give up the American Ballet Theater took a kind of courage that few of us ever show. Baryshnikov made his decision for one reason only: he felt he was still young enough to learn, and that this was his last chance to work with the two men he considered the world's greatest ballet masters, Balanchine and Robbins.

What happened was exactly what he had expected. He did indeed have a very hard time learning the new approach to his art. Some of his colleagues who saw him prepare for his first season at Saratoga say that he suffered almost continuously from tendonitis, a painful ailment that dancers fear, and that often afflicts them when they try new techniques. He was not eased into the New York City Ballet repertory gently. Of course, he danced some of the roles that seemed to be naturals for him: the exuberant, mischievous Franz in *Coppelia* and the funny, acrobatic Uncle Sam in *Stars and Stripes.* But by the time his first New York season began, he was assigned roles in some of Balanchine's most difficult ballets: *Orpheus,* with an intricate Stravinsky score, and *Four Temperaments* by Hindemith. In the beginning, and for the first time in his life, he got some very mixed reviews from dance critics, as well as disappointed reactions and reluctant applause from many of his former fans, who expected to see the flashy spins and jumps they had seen in *Turning Point.* Instead they saw the slow, carefully controlled movements of *Orpheus,* which seemed jagged, incomprehensible, angular and even ugly to someone accustomed to *Swan Lake* and *Giselle.*

Baryshnikov himself, in the beginning, seemed to have trouble with some of the ballets he was asked to do. In *Orpheus,* for instance, he not only had no bravura technical passages, he also wore a mask over his face for most of the performance and could not use his second most outstanding gift: his ability as a mime. With minimal movement of face and body, he was expected to create a mood of grief and despair, and at first, he obviously found this kind of subtle artistry difficult. But he danced *Orpheus* over and over again, much more often than he did the ballets that were clearly easier for him and for which he was consistently praised and applauded. By the time he gave his last *Orpheus* performance at the end of his first New York City Ballet season, he was heartbreakingly brilliant and, as he very well knew, there was not a reviewer in the house.

Apparently he can accept an unfavorable review and learn from it. Sometimes he is harder on himself than any critic, and his language is more picturesque. He felt like "a cow on ice" the first time he tried one unfamiliar ballet, he said. Another time he felt like "a fish in sand."

But while he was losing some of his former fans, he was acquiring a whole set of new ones. They buy the cheapest tickets, which is all they can afford. Young people, students, beginning professionals in engineering, accounting and law, as well as in art and architecture, really discovered Baryshnikov *after* he had resigned from superstardom. To them, the young man who did not seem to care what anybody thought about him had become a kind of hero, because they felt he had the qualities they admired most: integrity, a purity of purpose and, most of all, discipline. They applauded him most enthusiastically when he seemed to be failing because he had the courage to make mistakes. This new audience did not talk about "Misha's boyish charm," as those who had seen him in *Turning Point,* the TV shows, *Baryshnikov on Broadway* or *Baryshnikov in Hollywood,* and in his bravura performances at the American Ballet Theater did. Many of these young men and women had not gone to a ballet performance before. They went to see Baryshnikov not because they were the traditional ballet lovers, but because they recognized a role model when they saw one.

It is to these young people that Baryshnikov probably owes the honorary degree Yale University awarded him at the 1979 commencement exercises. He was the youngest person and the first dancer in anyone's memory to receive this award. The choice was wildly popular with Yale students, who generally regard honorary degree awards as a particularly boring part of graduation exercises. He received the kind of standing ovation that is usually reserved for other kinds of heroes or heroines. Actually Baryshnikov is also thought to be a favorite of Yale's young president, Bartlett Giamatti, a Renaissance scholar who, rumor goes, actually wrote the degree citation himself. (Usually these citations are written by a retired Yale historian.) It certainly summed up the feelings that many in Baryshnikov's new young audience would have found hard to express: "You have delighted lovers of ballet the world over with your glowing energy, grace, and technical mastery. You have brought classical dance to millions as you made your 'grande jetés' into their lives. With the courage of your conviction that artistic growth demands adventure, you have dared to let 'push come to shove' as you moved from Petipa to Tharp and Balanchine. Recognizing an imaginative choreographer and unparalleled dancer, Yale delights in conferring upon you the degree of Doctor of Fine Arts.''

A few weeks later, Baryshnikov surprised everyone again. The American Ballet company announced that in the fall of 1980, he would return to the fold, but not just as a principal dancer. He had been named artistic director, replacing both Lucia Chase and Oliver Smith who were resigning as of that time. Baryshnikov said little, danced all his scheduled performances with the New York City Ballet to the end of the season, told the press that he would continue with that company until he joined the American Ballet. This time he took a chance on losing his new, young audience. Many wondered whether, if paid a high enough price in money and power, he had not sold out after all. He had not.

In an interview before starting his new job, he made it very clear that he was rejoining the American Ballet Theater for exactly the same reason he had left it for the New York City Ballet: it now offered him opportunities to try out new skills: to direct, produce and teach, and to continue his influence on ballet when he no longer could dance at the top of his form. Here are some of the ideas and opinions he expressed in that interview:

On his new role with the American Ballet Theater: ''It was a very hard decision leaving the New York City Ballet, one of the most difficult I have ever made. There's still a lot I need to learn here. I'm very grateful to Mr. Balanchine and Mr. Robbins for letting me stay on that extra year. But running a company is a challenge, is so exciting. I can try new things, new techniques. I can find new, young dancers, new choreographers. And I'll stay in ballet after I'm too old to dance myself.''

On dancing and age: ''To you I'm very young, a kid, yes? But to dancers I'm almost an old man. One should stop when one's body won't do the job any more. Better to be anything than second-rate. In four years, when I'm 39, I'll probably have to stop performing. I'm not a maniac for the stage. But I'll still take classes, learn movements, work hard. Dancers have such a guilt to their bodies. It's like drinking too much wine or coffee. When

I take a day off, I just don't feel right. When I don't take class, I feel heavy like I have a lot of extra weight in my body. It's nice after exercising when the body is sweating a lot. You feel much lighter, better . . . much freer."

On fund-raising: "I don't know how and I won't do."

On the expected change in relationships to fellow dancers when he becomes management: "Everything changes. I have friends. They'll stay friends. But I will have to run a company. To do it right, I may have to decide many things . . . perhaps some will be angry, will like me less. But that's life. . . ." (Baryshnikov, like Balanchine, does not believe that ballet is a democracy.)

On taking vacations: "When I'm injured, I take time off, like right now. So, instead of taking classes, I'm talking to you. Even when I don't perform, I have to work . . . the body loses the ability to move, to do what one needs very quickly. By next week I'll be dancing again. Vacations are for writers . . . dancers can't stop for long."

On homesickness for Leningrad: "It gets less all the time. New York is my home now. I'll become an American citizen. Of course, I miss Leningrad . . . but that's life too. You live the way you must." (One symptom of his adaptation to his new country and language is when he talks to his dog, Kasha, half the time he now uses English. At the time of the interview Kasha was probably the only living being in Saratoga who understood Russian.)

On his Russian past: "I don't want to talk about that. I'm not a politician, I'm a dancer. Dancing is different here, life is different here. Contacts between people are different. You don't have to be afraid of telling the truth . . . fewer lies. One tells lies in Russia all the time. It's necessary. Also, I have to learn to trust people, including some I don't know well, like reporters. I feel freer here, but often sad. It's so stupid to have to leave one's home to be honest, to do what one wants and needs. Perhaps sometime that won't be necessary any more." (Baryshnikov's English has improved to the point where he understands subtle meanings of language. As a result, the word "defector" with its implication of disloyalty makes him wince. He is right. No one called Marlene Dietrich, or for that matter, Willy Brandt "defectors" from Nazi Germany. When Baryshnikov left Russia he was not "defecting" but seeking personal and artistic freedom. When he goes from one ballet company to another, he is not "defecting," just changing jobs.)

On self-discipline: "You can't stop. You can't be easy on yourself. You learn that early. Many very gifted dancers in Kirov School and School of American Ballet drop out at fifteen, sixteen. They don't want to live dancers' lives. Perhaps they are right. There are so many limits, so much we can't do. So much we miss. We run on nerves a lot. There's so much pressure. You must know when to start, and when to stop. If you don't, you get injured. And when you are injured, you don't dance. When you don't dance, you lose time, chances to learn, technique. Nobody is born to be a dancer. To be a dancer you must want it more than anything. You don't know in the beginning whether you will succeed. And then you don't know until later whether you will be injured and must stop. But you must live a disciplined life. The desire to be a dancer is the discipline of a career, and your work is the language of that discipline."

As he started yet another life in 1981, he, of course, needed all that self-discipline he talked about, in order to remake a company with a distinguished tradition and a cloudy present. He inherited a small number of highly paid superstars, and a disorganized, demoralized group of young corps dancers who had just gone through a bruising strike in order to obtain salaries that would permit them to survive in New York City. He also inherited a repertory, complete with scenery and costumes, that he would have to use for a few years, simply because there was not enough money to scrap existing pieces and start new ones. A new ballet may not cost as much as making a movie, but expenses can easily run into six figures.

What Baryshnikov had to do was work within some immovably set limits and to make the company look fresh and inspired. Few thought he could do it. By the end of 1981, some of the doubters were surprised at how well this very young man, with no training in organization and management, had succeeded. He used what he had learned in Russia, the impeccable training and technique, to improve the quality of the corps dancers. Then he used those same dancers in major roles, just as Balanchine had always done at the New York City Ballet. "No more excessively expensive foreign guest stars," he announced. The American Ballet Theater, from now on, would produce its own principal dancers. By 1982, the school that is affiliated with the company was revamped to produce the kinds of dancers the company needs, just as the School of American Ballet has always produced the kinds of dancers that fill the ranks of the New York City Ballet.

There were a few new pieces. There was an emphasis on doing the old classics better. But what almost everybody noticed was that, for the first time in years, the company looked like a company, not just like a loosely organized collection of dancers, some brilliant, some good, and some just barely competent.

Baryshnikov somehow managed to persuade the company's board of directors that, in spite of tight budgets, the dancers needed months instead of weeks of rehearsal time. They got that time, and during the 1981 season this produced results. There was, of course, also the fact that a good dancer could now expect to be picked for important solo roles, even though he or she might be spending his or her first year in the corps. This opportunity had always been open to New York City Ballet dancers, and apparently Baryshnikov saw that it was one of the secrets of that company's continued success and cohesiveness. Hardly anybody ever leaves the New York City Ballet. Almost everybody, at least in the corps, had left the American Ballet Theater after a few years. But with opportunities for advancement and artistic expression now available, corps members during the 1981 season outdid themselves. And Baryshnikov, in his new company, is clearly developing young dancers with star potential. Some already have a following among critics and regular audience members, although two years ago they were completely unknown.

Baryshnikov still has a lot of problems. He always will have, because there is also a flip side to many of the character traits that make him such an original and great artist. His integrity will make it difficult for him to compromise on principles. Artistic directors who are, after all, part of management, have usually found that compromises are necessary. His sharp intelligence is associated with a short attention span for anything he considers stupid or a waste of time. He is not a man to suffer fools gladly, but occasionally some fools may have a great deal of money to give to needy ballet companies. He has already indicated that the idea of fund-raising bores him. He hates crowds, parties, unless they are made up of congenial coworkers and others who interest him, and media attention by reporters he does not trust. Yet, obviously, one of the reasons he was asked to take the position he has accepted was that many hoped his name and presence would bring new money to the company. Also, because of all the attention he has received, there are some, in and out of the dance world, who resent him and insist his natural reticence is coldness or snobbery. As he takes on management functions and has to make those "hard decisions," this kind of criticism may increase.

Although he feels that as a dancer he is almost elderly, he is still a very young man. Almost inevitably he will be placed in situations in which there are older people under him and this too may prove to be difficult.

Before the start of many of his performances, a "bag lady" regular circulates outside the theater. She asks if anyone has an extra ticket they might be willing to give her. If she can't get one, she often turns up in the standing room section, bags and all. One evening, after Baryshnikov had taken his last curtain call, she called out to him: "Have a good life, Misha." She has a point. One might well wish that for this brilliant, complicated, rootless, disciplined, serious, amusing, sometimes imperious, and frequently solitary young-old man.

But having a good life may mean something different to a dedicated dancer. Instead of leisure, it may mean more hard work. Instead of more freedom, it may mean coping better with limitations. And instead of finding a safe spot in life, it may mean more challenges, changes and adventures. Life does not get easier for dancers as they get older. Usually, it gets harder. Baryshnikov seems to know this and accept it. Overcoming difficulties has been his specialty most of his life.

CHAPTER XIX

Peter Martins

Principal dancers in the New York City Ballet have triumphed in their profession, but they have not escaped it. Grueling physical work is a daily necessity . . . stress is ubiquitous. Principals have more time away from the company, more time in which to think and to complicate their lives. . . .

    —JOSEPH H. MAZO in *Dance Is a Contact Sport.*

"I probably would have left the ballet world if it hadn't been for this company. Because it doesn't interest me . . . the other ballet world. There's no focus . . . no direction. . . . It's more like a business. And if I were going to be a businessman, I'd find some other business than dance. Dance, among other things, is not a very lucrative business. . . ."

    —PETER MARTINS in an interview.

P ETER MARTINS is a full-time dancer who, in the few hours a week and the few weeks a year that are truly his own, is also trying to turn himself into a full-time choreographer. He thinks a lot. Whether the thinking complicates his life or enriches it, only he can know.

Like several of the NYCB principal male dancers, he was born and trained in Denmark. By the time he was eighteen years old, he was already well-known in his own country as an outstanding member of the Royal Danish Ballet. But he was restless even then. "Denmark is a small country," he says. "Everything is small there. Only one ballet company. Only a small audience. America seemed so big. Lots of space. Lots of companies. If I could make it there, I thought, I would really have made it. I was always ambitious. . . ."

The opportunity to come to the United States arrived unexpectedly, and an invitation from George Balanchine to audition for the role of "Apollo." NYCB was dancing at the Edinburgh Festival in Scotland. The dancer who had been scheduled to dance the role had been injured. There were only two other dancers in the world who could, perhaps, perform it on short notice. One of these was on tour in South America. The other was Peter Martins, who had danced Apollo that season with the Royal Danish Ballet.

Even at age eighteen, Martins was not asked to audition for a role. He already had his choice of parts in the Danish company. And, as he tells it, he was not exactly thrilled about traveling to Scotland on the chance that he just might be chosen to do a part he had already done to critical acclaim in his own country. Yet, although he had never met Balanchine, he had seen enough of his work to respect him more than any other choreographer. So he went to Scotland, did the audition, got the role and, then and there, reached a turning point in his life.

When Balanchine asked him to join the New York Company, he immediately agreed. Some of his older Danish colleagues told him to think over the proposal more carefully. After all, he would be leaving a secure job, with a guaranteed pension, when he left the Royal Danish Ballet. "At the time, it seemed silly to talk to a eighteen-year-old about retirement," Martins says now. "As a matter of fact, it still seems silly. If you want security, you don't become a dancer."

He was married to a Danish dancer, and they had a young son. His family stayed in Denmark. They are still there. The son is studying dance at the Royal Danish Ballet School and has performed children's roles with the company. Once, several years ago, members of that company came to New York for a series of recitals. Martins danced in one piece with his son. They look remarkably alike.

Martins was bound to be noticed by the New York ballet audience. He joined the company as a principal, something that rarely happens to so young a dancer. He is a spectacular looking man, with a powerful six-foot-two-inch body and wide shoulders narrowing down to a small waist. His hair is the color of wheat, and his eyes are ice-blue. Sometimes his face can look as if it were sculpted for a statue of Apollo by an early Greek artist. At other times, he can look like the kind of hero an eleven-year-old girl will dream of after spending an evening reading tales of ancient romances. And because he can be so dazzling just standing still, many tended to look at just the man, rather than at the already highly accomplished dancer.

What's more, for Balanchine, the principal dancer in most ballets is usually not the man, but the ballerina. "Ballet is woman," he has said. And Martins was used often just to provide a particularly handsome backdrop for the ballerina. Partnering is a special skill, and Martins is a master of it, but it does not get noticed as much as solo variations complete with spectacular jumps and air turns.

Also, the Balanchine repertory, in the beginning, gave Martins more trouble than he had expected. There is a reason why most of the top male dancers in the world tend to be fairly small and, often, slight. It is harder for a tall, big man to dance ballet. He needs more strength to get himself into the air, for one thing. And big men have to be faster than smaller men to look as if they were moving at a similar speed.

Actually much of the training Martins had received in Denmark was helpful and eventually made it possible for him to become one of the best of all Balanchine's male dancers. The Royal Danish Ballet trains its company in the methods and roles of August Bournonville, a nineteenth-century choreographer, who for decades was artistic director of that company. Bournonville, like Balanchine, emphasized speed, agility and exact musical timing. A dancer trained in Denmark may find it easier to learn the Balanchine style and method than a dancer trained only in Russian or French classical ballet.

In the beginning, however, Martins did not find it easy to turn himself into a Balanchine dancer. For a while, he was not

even sure he wanted to be one. His looks and his classical training made it possible for him to get well-paid guest roles with
other companies, and he took those opportunities. He realized
that he could make a great deal more money as a guest performer,
jetting all over the globe, than as a dancer in one company that,
he quickly realized, required a total commitment. But as he
learned more from and about Balanchine, he came to respect and
even revere him. He learned the roles that Balanchine had made
for other dancers, and eventually mastered them better than any
man in the company.

Eventually, for the Stravinsky Festival in 1972, Balanchine
made two roles especially for him: *Violin Concerto* and *Duo
Concertante.* During the time that Martins came to know the
special qualities of Balanchine's choreographies, Balanchine apparently also came to know Martins's special physical and emotional capacities. Although other dancers have performed in
works made for Martins by Balanchine, they never look totally
right. He is one of those dancers who makes a role his own, and
to whom every other performer who attempts the same choreography will always be compared.

Something else happened. Balanchine started to pair Martins
with the most spectacular ballerina in the company: Suzanne
Farrell. (See Chapter XX.) When those two dance together, they
produce the kind of sparks that can light up a stage. They have
never been close personally, but, as dancing partners, they are
more than a perfect match; they bring out special qualities in
each other. Martins, though brilliant, can be a cool and somewhat detached performer. Farrell, who is tall and big-boned for a
dancer, looks fragile, even vulnerable with him. His technical
abilities seem to challenge hers. Neither ever looks better than
when they are dancing with each other. And neither knows why
this is so. Both suspect that Balanchine does. They don't attempt
to analyze what happens to them on stage.

Martins is now in his middle thirties. With Baryshnikov,
who is one of his best friends, he may be one of the two top male
ballet stars in the world today—and this has happened to Martins
in a company that keeps repeating, year after year, that it has no
stars, nor any interest in creating any. He has held that position
long enough so that now, occasionally, he indicates that he is a
little bored with dancing.

In fact, he says that he never had the overwhelming urge to

be on stage that so many other performers have. In a way, he has always been a little uncomfortable as a dancer. He is a very private person, and even when he maintains his cool and analytical detachment on stage, he still says he feels that when the curtain goes up, someone has pulled up a blind to reveal a part of his personality that he prefers to keep hidden. Apparently he does not really crave having people, either in an audience or on a street, look at him. Most performers do—that's why they become actors or dancers in the first place.

Martins, however, is not at all uncomfortable doing choreography, even though the dances he creates reveal more about him than the choreographies he dances. His first piece, *Calcium Light Night*, is, he says, a completely plotless ballet, a dance about dancing. It starts with a boy wandering onto an empty stage . . . possibly after a performance, with only the bright light shining on center stage that is left after everyone has gone home. Martins said that the picture in his mind, when he created this first of many choreographies was exactly that: the dancer coming back, perhaps to pick up something, after the house was empty. "Do you realize that almost as soon as the curtain goes down on a performance, it comes right back up again?" he asks. "It's a picture that stays in one's mind. There were thousands of people in that theater, perhaps twenty minutes ago. The curtain goes down . . . and a few minutes later comes up again, with only that light on stage. Perhaps that was what I was trying to catch in those first steps in *Calcium*."

But the ballet, made for dancers Heather Watts and Daniel Duell to a few short pieces by American composer Charles Ives, shows a great deal about those two dancers and their interaction. There is something of the divided feelings that Martins apparently has about his own dancing in the first hesitant steps and later in the highly energetic variations of the boy on stage. There is also something about the nervous energy and tension found in many Balanchine ballerinas in the variations he created for Watts. When the two dancers finally meet for a series of pas de deux, sparks fly. The couple collides. They separate. They sling each other around the stage. The male dancer is not, strictly speaking, a partner. He does not hold up the girl. If anything, they hold each other up . . . and topple each other over.

When Martins was asked by a reviewer whether the relationship between the boy and girl in the dance was "one of love or its opposite," he thought for a second and answered: "What's the difference?"

If *Calcium* is indeed about dancing, and certainly the choreographer should know what he meant to convey, then it may also be about the relationship that Martins himself has with his own profession.

He may take himself very seriously as a choreographer, but he does not now, nor apparently ever has been able to, take himself seriously as a celebrity. Until very recently, he bicycled to work from his apartment and parked his bike in the back of a somewhat scrungy coffee shop opposite the New York State Theater. Dancers are not supposed to risk life and limb biking along Broadway. He says that he answers all fan mail from girls up to about the age of ten, because when he was that age, he was madly in love with Debbie Reynolds and wrote her for an autographed picture. She never answered his letter (presumably written in recently-learned English, rather than Danish) and that hurt his feelings. He doesn't want to hurt his ten-year-old fans, he says.

He works well and easily with young people and has done several ballets for the students of the School of American Ballet. Before a recent performance, he was trying to teach a very young boy, who came up to about his waist, that it was more important to come down on the right note than to turn an extra time in the air. "Do it this way," he said, doing a turn and a half and hitting the ground in exact time to the music. "They always applaud me when I do this . . . don't worry, they'll applaud you too."

He has done many ballets since *Calcium*, for the school and the company. Some show Balanchine's influence more than others. In a way, it is difficult for a choreographer as gifted as Martins to be always considered a dancer first and, when he decides to make dances of his own, to be compared invariably to the greatest choreographer of this century: Balanchine.

If he were working for any other company but NYCB, perhaps those comparisons would not be made so persistently. There are many choreographers who do work not nearly as original as Martins for companies all over the world, and they are rarely compared to Balanchine. But NYCB is where Martins now works, and where he will probably remain in the foreseeable future. He is the only male dancer in that company who, at this time, cannot be replaced. There are roles that just can't be danced by anyone else effectively. That's partly due to Martins's size. In some pieces in the NYCB repertory, he provides a needed focus simply because he is so big and visible. But more than any other male dancer in the world, he understands the Balanchine repertory and, therefore, can teach it as well as dance it. In recognition of this fact, he was named the fourth ballet master, with Balanchine, Robbins and John Taras, in the fall of 1981.

So, for the time being, he will be dancing and teaching and will attempt in those few minutes a day, and the even fewer days in a week that are his own, to make the choreographies he wants to do so badly. He has also said that, since the age of fourteen, he has wanted to manage his own company. There are those who say that eventually, when Balanchine is no longer on the scene, Martins may be his successor. But there are others who say that Balanchine cannot have a successor. That he *is* the New York City Ballet.

Meanwhile, Martins has taken a small group of NYCB dancers, mostly corps members, on the road, once with Baryshnikov and once by himself. Both tours, which went to several European cities as well as parts of the United States, were financially and artistically successful. He has also been offered the directorship of at least one established company, which he turned down.

Whatever happens, it is reasonable to suppose that eventually Martins will be running a company, one that is molded by his own personality and talents, rather than by the image of one created by the man he loves and admires beyond all others, but in whose shadow he has always felt he stood. Whether that company is the New York City Ballet, or something called "Peter Martins and Friends," Martins has enough to offer as a dancer, teacher and choreographer to learn all he can from his mentor, Balanchine, and then to find his own direction and goals as an artist.

CHAPTER XX

Suzanne Farrell

Dancing doesn't get any easier. But I have standards that are very high and they depend on George Balanchine. I like him to be proud. You can't let the public be your measure. It pleases when the audience appreciates me, but I really dance for myself . . . and for God.

—SUZANNE FARRELL in an interview published in the magazine *Quest: The Pursuit of Excellence.*

O NE HAS to have watched Suzanne Farrell dance to understand what she means when she says she dances for God. She is known to be devoutly religious, but the God for whom she dances is probably not the same one she worships at Mass. It's a kind of mysterious power that she feels inside herself and that becomes visible to her audiences only when she dances.

If one sees her on the street, usually in rehearsal clothes, her long hair tucked under a wool cap in winter, or tied with a ribbon in summer, her face bare of make-up, she might easily pass unnoticed: a tall, good-looking woman in a hurry. When she steps on the stage, she seems to walk into another world in which there is no audience, no orchestra pit, no scenery: just a mysterious realm she has created for herself. Many of the dances Balanchine has made for her bring out that special mystery that surrounds her, and that makes her unlike any other woman dancer who has stepped out on any stage, anywhere.

Suzanne Farrell was born Sue Ann Flicker in 1945, in Cincinnati. Her mother was divorced early and supported herself as a nurse, doing night duty most of the time so that she could spend her days with her three daughters. Apparently what she wanted for them was careers in the arts. The oldest, Donna, studied ballet, the second, Beverly, the piano. Sue started accompanying Donna to ballet class when she was a toddler. She began ballet herself when she was eight. One can only imagine how difficult life must have been for the mother, trying to provide three daughters with the best artistic training available, on the salary of a night nurse.

Like so many dancers, Sue knew very early that she wanted to be a dancer. She even knew in what company: the New York City Ballet, which she had seen in a performance in her home town. With her sisters and a close friend, she would put on dance performances in her living room. Her hero was NYCB dancer Jacques d'Amboise, whose role was usually taken by an armchair in the ballets Sue dreamed up for her at-home performances.

"Sue Flicker worked seriously but joyously; joy was to remain the particular component of her dancing, mounting sometimes to ecstasy," wrote Olga Maynard in an article in *Dance* magazine in 1979. "The studio and the stage were absolutes of existence; dancing the intimate reality. She passed through adolescence like a little nun."

When Sue was fourteen, her mother realized that she would need better training than any available to her in Cincinnati. She moved herself and her family to New York City. At fifteen, Sue auditioned for the School of American Ballet and was one of the first to be accepted on that organization's then-new Ford Foundation scholarship.

At the school, Sue Flicker disappeared and Suzanne Farrell emerged. She got her name from the Manhattan telephone directory. It had the kind of poetic sound she liked . . . and, as it turned out, it suited her perfectly. It's not a theatrical name, but a melodious, elegant one: American with slightly Continental overtones.

By the time she had turned sixteen, she was a member of the

ballet company and, as has happened so often, before and since, was given her first leading role while still a member of the corps. A principal dancer fell ill, and Sue (now Suzanne) danced her first solo in Balanchine's *Serenade*. She was noticed immediately. Her qualities as a dancer, both technical and personal, made her unique from the start. She had less than a day to prepare for her debut, but she showed a quality she has often demonstrated since: she is a fast learner who can give a technically perfect performance after a few rehearsals, but who continues to polish every step, every movement continuously, sometimes over a period of years.

"You never have enough time to prepare for a role," she told an interviewer. "You have to learn a role through the music and depend on it to tell you exactly where you should be. Only then are you free to be spontaneous." That statement could have been made by Balanchine. There are definite points of similarity in the natures of the great dancer and the great choreographer: their respect, bordering on reverence, for music, and their innate mysticism, to name just two.

Balanchine apparently was more fascinated with Farrell than he had been with any other dancer in his company. He created one role after another for her. Among the first was a pas de deux in which she was paired with the hero of her childhood: Jacques d'Amboise. Now she was dancing with the real man . . . no longer with a chair. But she found the ballet difficult, not technically, but emotionally. "It was all about being in love, and I had never been in love," she said. If she had not experienced the actuality of love, she must have been able to imagine the feeling. Imagining feelings has always been one of her greatest strengths. At any rate, the ballet was a huge success and has remained in the repertory ever since. The only two dancers who have ever been cast in it are Farrell and d'Amboise. It is one of the few dances he still performs.

D'Amboise became her regular partner. For one thing, he was tall enough for her. For another, their styles seemed to suit each other. Not until Peter Martins appeared on the scene many years later was there a man who could bring out and contrast, her special personal qualities as a dancer. D'Amboise was lighthearted, spirited, extroverted. Farrell, then as now, was mystical, serious, looking inside herself more than at the real world.

For eight years, she danced principal roles with NYCB, many

of them created especially for her by Balanchine. In 1965, he made a version of *Don Quixote* for her . . . she was Dulcinea, the heroine who never existed and whom the Don worshipped. Balanchine performed the Don himself . . . the last time he was to appear on stage.

In 1969, she married a dancer from the company. Both left shortly after the marriage. They moved to Belgium and joined a company that was exceedingly controversial even then: choreographer Maurice Béjart's Ballet of the Twentieth Century. Béjart is a very different choreographer from Balanchine. Where Balanchine emphasizes pure line and movement, strict attention to music and, usually, elimination of story content, Béjart's ballets are big and splashy with sensational costumes, often strange make-up, flashing lights and elaborate scenery. He tends to reinterpret the ballets of other choreographers, and sometimes, reverses sex roles. For instance, the Firebird, in all other ballets done to the Stravinsky score, is always a woman. In Béjart's ballet, the bird is a man.

His work and Farrell's style never really suited each other. By 1975, Farrell was back with the NYCB, the only dancer who had ever left the company, and was welcomed back by Balanchine. This is how dance critic Arlene Croce describes her return in her book, *Afterimages:* "Suzanne Farrell, one of the great dancers of the age, has rejoined the New York City Ballet. She returned without publicity, entering the stage on Peter Martins's arm in the adagio movement of the Balanchine-Bizet *Symphony in C.* As a long bourrée (a series of very short steps on point) to the oboe solo began, the audience withheld its applause as if wanting to be sure that this was indeed Suzanne Farrell. Then a thunderclap, lasting perhaps fifteen seconds, rolled around the theater, ending as decisively as it had begun, and then there fell the deeper and prolonged silence of total absorption. For the next eight minutes, nobody except the dancers moved a muscle. . . ."

Farrell was back with the company and has been there ever since. She dances some of the ballets Balanchine made for her, and several new ones, added since her return. She can be everything from a passionate Gypsy in *Tzigane* to a death-haunted girl in *La Valse.* Some of her former roles are now danced by other, younger dancers, but to several she brings that unique quality that seems to make her irreplaceable. Among those roles would seem to be the last movement of Balanchine's tribute to the art of the waltz and to turn-of-the-century Europe: *Vienna Waltzes.* When it was first performed, many critics looked on it as just another pretty waltz ballet, a part of a continued love affair Balanchine seems to have with that particular dance form. For four sections, this may be true. But everything changes in the last section. To the music of Richard Strauss, Farrell slowly moves alone into a dimly lit ballroom. Dressed in a long white satin ball gown, she dances with her back to the audience, her front appearing as a reflection in the mirrors that line the room. She waltzes off slowly, dreamily, totally self-absorbed. A male dancer in black evening clothes joins her, takes her in his arms, dances with her around the stage and then disappears, as mysteriously as he came. Farrell again dances alone . . . seemingly looking and longing for some unseen and unreachable person or goal: perhaps a phantom lover, perhaps something entirely different. The man reappears and dances with her again. Farrell seems to swoon in his arms. Whoever the phantom is, she has fallen in love with him. He leaves her, dancing out into the wings. Looking as if she has seen a ghost, she dances offstage slowly.

Every time she does this, the audience is breathless. No one applauds. Whatever it is that is haunting Farrell casts its spell over everyone. Once, as she was coming offstage, she said to another dancer: "I feel that I have been dancing with death." The dancer reported that her face looked as if, indeed, she had.

After Farrell disappears into the wings, the waltz music changes. It becomes faster, gayer, louder. The chandeliers, which have thrown out only a muted bluish light, brighten to gold. The entire company reappears on stage, all the women dressed in white satin, the men in evening clothes. They whirl around the floor, sometimes all couples together, sometimes a few singled out. Farrell and her partner are in the middle. Now they look like a couple dancing a waltz at a ball. The mysterious overtones are gone . . . everything is bright and sunny again.

The last section of *Vienna Waltzes* is like one of those ink blot tests that psychologists give their patients to find out how they interpret the figures the blots seem to make. Almost everyone sees something different in this ballet. But the sense of mystery that Farrell's solo and pas de deux engender remains long after one has left the theater. What are Balanchine and Farrell saying? Only they know . . . and Farrell, like her mentor, also doesn't think one can explain a flower.

CHAPTER XXI

Patricia McBride

Patricia McBride, who gained principal dancer status a few years before Farrell, didn't become a star until just a few years ago. She didn't have Farrell's grandeur or silky, rippling flow of movement; she had a little stick-like body, which she has patiently taught to move deeply and expansively . . . If Farrell was shy, McBride was shyer. Even today, she is the shyest, most tenderly true, bravest and least corruptible of classical dancers. But it's just by having been these things, night after night for ten solid years, that she has fought her way to distinction.

—ARLENE CROCE, in a piece written in 1971, and included in *Afterimages.*

Poll a sample of the company's dancing children and you'll find Patricia McBride is almost every little girl's favorite grown-up ballerina. "She has time for kids." "She let my grandmother take my picture with her." "She's nice." The esteem is mutual. "Of course, I have time for the kids," says McBride, smiling at the thought. "They relax me."

—ANNE MURPHY in *Ballet News.*

DURING THE 1981 spring season, Patricia McBride was spending her twenty-second year with the New York City Ballet, her twentieth as a principal dancer. Early in her career, Balanchine had made several ballets for her. During the Farrell years, she had continued to dance, often every evening, with two ballets on matinee days. But all the new choreographies were for Farrell. There is no way that she could not have felt hurt by her apparent loss of status. Even in 1981, as she talked about those years, there was some pain in her voice. Like all of the Balanchine dancers, her professional world, since the beginning, has revolved around him. His approval was what she needed more than the applause that she invariably received from the audience.

During the years that Farrell was not in the company, Mc-Bride came back into her own. Many felt that, in her own inconspicuous way, she held the company together. The first ballet Balanchine made, two years after Farrell's departure, was *Who Cares?* to music by George Gershwin, and it had an important role for McBride in it, one that presented her in an entirely new light. She danced American jazz, on point, in a style that reminded moviegoers of Ginger Rogers. "I'd *love* to see Pat dance with Fred Astaire," remarked her husband, dancer Jean-Pierre Bonnefous, then a principal in the NYBC.

McBride was also the ballerina on whom Balanchine set his most successful story ballet, *Coppelia* (score by Delibes), a deceptively simple little story about a young couple in a sunny village who are to be married. But their future happiness is threatened by the fact that the future bridegroom, a rambunctious youth called Franz, seems to fall in love with every pretty girl in sight, including a lifelike mechanical doll created by a self-deluded magician, Dr. Coppelius.

Coppelius, who carefully locks up his studio, one day is accosted by Franz and friends, who tease him mercilessly. He loses the key to his house. Swanilda, the fiancée, finds it, and with *her* friends invades the studio and makes several of the mechanical toys dance. They find the doll, Coppelia, behind a curtain just as Coppelius returns and chases the girls away. Swanilda stays, changes her clothes with those on the doll, and manages to fool the magician. At this point, Franz climbs in through a window to see for himself what Coppelia really looks like. Coppelius catches him and, at first, attempts to give him a sound thrashing. He changes his mind, however, and instead, invites Franz, who seems to like liquor almost as much as he likes girls, for a drink. The drink has a sleeping draught in it. Coppelius, reading a large and mysterious-looking book, thinks he has found a formula to turn his doll into a real-life woman by transferring some of a person's qualities to the toy. He attempts to draw from Franz the life forces and to install them into the doll. Swanilda goes along with the game.

Much to his delight, he seems to have turned the toy into a person, but she quickly makes him wish he had never tried the experiment. Willfully, she wrecks his studio, pushing over the other toys and, in every way showing Coppelius that she is not even slightly interested in him. Her interest is only for the sleeping Franz. As Franz begins to awake, Coppelius tries to push Swanilda into the doll's alcove. She vanishes briefly and returns carrying the broken body of the doll, naked and wigless. Franz is by now aware of his foolish infatuation with the doll, and he and Swanilda leave the studio, mocking the old man who looks brokenly at his favorite creation.

In the last act, there is a village festival. Coppelius is given money by the mayor to recompense him for the damage done by the young people. Franz and Swanilda get married, and the celebration starts with many divertissements (special solo dances for a variety of characters). The last dance, called "Peace," is a stunning pas de deux for Swanilda and Franz, one of the most difficult and acrobatic in the Balanchine repertory.

The story seems sweet and harmless enough . . . the kind of ballet to which one would take one's favorite eight-year-old niece. And, of course, there are a lot of children in the audience (as well as on the stage, in several of those divertissements) when the ballet is performed.

But like everything by Balanchine, nothing is as simple as it seems. The *Coppelia* story is actually based on a tragic fairy tale by a Romantic German writer, E. T. A. Hoffman, in which the discovery of the deception destroys the magician, and in which the characters of Swanilda and Franz are anything but sunny and lovable.

If one looks carefully at the Balanchine version, there are

distinct overtones of this tragedy in his story, too. Franz and his friends seem cruel as they taunt the old man in the street. The young man's fascination with girls and drink does not bode well for the marriage. Neither does Swanilda's jealousy, her willfulness and her final malicious joke on Dr. Coppelius. Everything may be sunny on that wedding day for the two lovers, but one hopes that the village in which the story takes place has a marriage counseling agency. Swanilda and Franz don't look as if they are destined for a long and happy marriage.

No one can bring out the dual nature of Swanilda, the charm and fun mixed with the willfulness and cruelty, as well as McBride. Of all the American-born, American-trained ballerinas in this company, she is the one who has, apparently, a real gift as an actress as well as a dancer. And if she knows how to act, she taught herself those skills. There is almost no other Balanchine ballet that requires the kind of subtle characterization that makes *Coppelia* so effective.

As one talks to McBride, it becomes evident that her stage personality is different from her real one. She is just as shy as Croce indicated. The shyness shows in her soft, girlish voice and her retiring manner. But, on stage, she sparkles. Some dance critics have said that, for a true ballerina, McBride lacks the quality they call "mystery," that special elusiveness that is part of Farrell's nature and stage personality. On stage, McBride indeed has very little mystery. She presents herself as clear and fresh as a spring of water. She may dance for God and Balanchine, like Farrell, but most of all, she dances for the members of her audience. As Coppelia, she flirts with them, she takes them into her confidence, she makes them part of the action. But the private McBride is a mixture of many qualities, some obvious, some hidden.

"I'm a very strong person," she said in a magazine interview for a story on how some women deal with extreme physical and emotional stress that is an inevitable part of her work. At the time of the interview, she was dancing in spite of a foot injury, simply because she was needed. At five-feet-three-inches, weighing somewhere in the neighborhood of ninety pounds, she looks so fragile as to seem almost transparent. But, of course, she is correct in her claim of strength. Only a very strong woman could, after twenty years, still manage her brutal schedule. Actually, that look of frailty is part of every ballerina's stock in trade, and

it works especially well for McBride. The appearance of a snowflake combined with the strength and stamina of a football quar-
terback, is the essential ingredient of McBride's success, along
with a serenity and a genuinely sunny disposition that endears
her to those dancing children and many of her coworkers as well.
"Pat doesn't have a mean bone in that ninety-pound body of
hers," says dancer Lourdes Lopez. Bart Cook, another principal
in the company, told an interviewer of the time in Paris when he
had to dance a particularly taxing Balanchine choreography while
"deathly sick with dysentery." "Patty just said, 'Don't worry, I'll
get you through.' On stage she kept talking and joking with me
—she even tickled me—and I forgot my troubles and actually
gave one of my better performances. But she's the one who got
me through it," he said.

While Baryshnikov was with NYCB, McBride was his regular
partner. She was the right size for him . . . most of the other
Balanchine ballerinas were too tall. But that was not the only
reason why she was paired with the Russian, known for his speed
and agility. Part of the reason was that Baryshnikov also needed
help to be "gotten through" some of the many new choreographies he was assigned. Some of those roles were exceedingly difficult for him. McBride often made him look wonderful, although
some always seemed to think that *he* was the one who made *her*
look terrific. This could not have been an easy time for her.

During those seasons, she was working with a foot that had
been injured a year before and that did not heal completely until
a year later. It was the kind of injury that is a dancer's nightmare.
Her foot hurt the night she danced for Jimmy Carter and his
family (and for a nationwide TV audience) at the White House. It
hurt when she danced a ballet with only a few hours of rehearsal
time, which she had not performed for several seasons, because
the program had to be changed at the last minute when Baryshnikov was injured. It hurt when she charmed the audience into a
standing ovation on a night when groans of disappointment
greeted the company because of an announcement, just before
curtain time, that the still injured Baryshnikov would not appear
in the principal role of *Harlequinade*, which had become one of
his specialties, and that he would be replaced by a relatively
unknown performer. She got that young dancer, understandably
nervous about replacing the legendary Russian, through the per-

formance too . . . with almost no one in the audience realizing what she was doing.

None of the stress she must have felt during those busy seasons were ever evident on stage. Nor was the fact that she and Baryshnikov were not well-suited partners, temperamentally or in dance style. But the stress was often clearly visible offstage as she sat in her dressing room and tiredly took off her ballet slippers, rubbed her ankle and removed her make-up. Still, on one such evening, she spent an extra hour giving an interview she had promised, which she easily could have postponed. As everybody in the company knows, McBride keeps her commitments.

She answered questions about how she deals with stress. How did she manage her almost impossible schedule? How did she deal with pain, fear, exhaustion, all daily parts of her life? "Good heredity, good nutrition in early childhood and habits of discipline that form a necessary part of ballet," she said. "I come from very strong stock. What's more, my mother and my grandmother were nutrition buffs long before it became fashionable. When I was a child, there simply was no junk food in the house —no soda pop, no potato chips, no store-bought candy, cookies or cake. Just fresh fruit, vegetables, juice and milk. We ate a lot of fish and chicken. My German grandmother opposed convenience foods on principle . . . everything was made from scratch, including the soup that was the standard first course at every meal."

Those basic diet habits have remained with her, although now, somewhat guiltily, she drinks gallons of cola a week, because she feels it gives her a fast energy boost. Possibly because of her early nutrition habits, she has never had a weight problem; instead she worries about becoming too thin by the end of a ballet season. Other dancers may have to diet constantly, including her husband, who after many years as a member of the New York City Ballet has retired from dancing, because of injuries, to devote his time to choreography. (He recently was commissioned to do a version of Stravinsky's *Rite of Spring* for the Metropolitan Opera.) It's interesting that she and her husband rarely go out for meals. She does most of the cooking . . . like her grandmother, whose sturdy spirit she seems to have inherited along with her nutrition philosophy, she distrusts convenience and restaurant food.

In the general atmosphere of crisis, verging on mild hysteria, that seems to invade all dance companies, including the NYCB, backstage, McBride's dressing room seems like an island of serenity. "I've always been a rather calm person," she says, "but my marriage has helped me a lot. It's wonderful that my husband and I are in the same profession, that we can help each other through difficult situations, comfort each other, encourage each other and really talk out our professional problems together. He is my best friend as well as my husband."

Over the years, company members say, Bonnefous has also helped her overcome some of her extreme shyness, which is still evident in her voice. "I have sometimes become so frightened going onstage in a new ballet that I didn't think I could make it," she said. "I still get stage fright, and I'm usually a little uncomfortable meeting a whole crowd of people, but a happy marriage helps a lot." Some of the dancers in the company who know her best say that, in recent years, she has also become a little more assertive, more insistent on having some of her rights, including those for more free time, respected.

During the 1981–82 winter season, she did not dance. Her name was listed as a principal in the program, but she was not scheduled for any ballets. Many of her fans worried about her. Was their favorite Coppelia, their favorite *Nutcracker*'s Sugar Plum Fairy seriously injured? After all, by now she had danced for almost twenty-five years. It turned out that she was pregnant, and the news seemed to please everyone in the audience and backstage as much as if a member of their own family had suddenly announced that she was going to have a baby. A year ago, Bonnefous and McBride had adopted a Korean orphan, apparently because they felt that they might not be able to have children of their own. In 1982, they did, after all, have their own son. Most company members expect McBride to remain part of the company now that the child is born, although she may reduce her exhausting dancing schedule a great deal. "Pat loves ballet . . . she loves Balanchine, and she loves this company," said one young corps member. "In some capacity, she will probably be with us for years." And all the stage mothers, helping their little daughters into *Nutcracker* costumes, nodded in enthusiastic agreement. Everybody felt that, for once, a truly nice person had really finished *first*, in her personal as well as in her professional life.

CHAPTER XXII

Natalia Makarova

Tradition is integral to the ballerina's art. From it she moves forward to deploy her own performing gifts, but conscious of the essential laws of stylistic expression. Thus Makarova's Giselle, Odette/Odile [in Swan Lake]*, Aurora [in* Sleeping Beauty] *are extensions of the great achievements of her great predecessors . . . the history of the Imperial Ballet in St. Petersburg is implicit in her performances.*

—British critic CLEMENT CRISP
discussing Makarova's style in *Ballet News.*

She's not only taken a masterpiece of choreography, she's taken the American Ballet Theater's corps—hardly the most sensitive instrument in the world, and recharged it from top to bottom. In place of the lifeless, gray ensemble that has skated through Giselle *and* Swan Lake *all these many years, there is now in* La Bayadere *an alert, disciplined and expressive corps de ballet, trembling with self-discovery.*

—ARLENE CROCE in a review of Makarova's restaging
of a Petipa ballet, included in *Afterimages.*

NATALIA MAKAROVA left the Kirov Company, which at the time was performing in London, via the stage door and never returned. She is the only woman among the Kirov and Bolshoi defectors who has become a star dancer in the United States and Europe. Other women have left too, but they are virtually unknown to the ballet-going public, although many were excellent dancers in the classical Russian style.

As a dancer, Makarova is unique in that she carries with her, more than any of the other Russians who have come to the West, the style and tradition of Petipa and the Imperial Russian Ballet. She talks wistfully about the fact that few new ballets have been created for her by American and European choreographers; but her real strength, both as a dancer and as one who stages dances, is rootedness in the past. If someone wished to build, stone by stone, and step by step, an exact replica of the Maryinski at Lincoln Center, they could find no better architect than this paper-thin, seemingly fragile ballerina who, according to all who know her, has a will and determination of iron.

Balanchine is also rooted in the Maryinski, but he has used those roots as a base on which to build a new kind of dance. Makarova does not seem to want to change the dance traditions under which she grew and blossomed. She wants to take those Petipa ballets, which now often look dusty and worn, pull them apart, piece by piece, shine all the pieces to a diamond gloss and then put the whole choreography back together again. It's obvious she feels that the line of dancers that stretches from the Maryinski to the present and into the future must be preserved, the way rare and beautiful icons, the Russian paintings of saints, are preserved. Indeed, icons decorate her apartments in San Francisco and New York.

Her personal life has, of course, changed dramatically since she left her former country and company to become one of the top ballet stars of the West. Not only is she a principal dancer with the American Ballet Theater, and with fellow Kirov alumnus, Baryshnikov, one of that company's principal attractions, she has also married an American, Edward Karkar, a San Francisco businessman, and has a son, born in this country in 1978.

She calls André, "my greatest creation." He also has what might be considered one of the most distinguished sets of godparents in the world. They include exiled King Constantine of Greece, Jacqueline Kennedy Onassis and the dancer Rudolf Nureyev.

In 1980, she attempted her own experiment in capitalism. She formed a dance company that was supposed to be not only self-supporting, but profit-making. The experiment did not work. If it proved anything, it was that her instinctive leaning toward tradition was entirely correct. One cannot create an instant ballet company any more than an instant city, or even a very good instant souffle. Dancers need to work together, to experiment with choreography together, to establish professional and personal relationships, to develop slowly, keeping what's good and weeding out what's bad over a period of many years.

Makarova booked some very fine dancers, Americans as well as European, as guest artists. She formed and trained herself a young corps de ballet. She attempted to dance at every performance, since she was, after all, the attraction that ticket buyers were expecting. But somehow, the enterprise never jelled. Makarova herself, even though she was still recovering from a knee operation, looked terrific most of the time. Many of her guests looked very good, too. But they also seemed like a group of strangers who had met, accidentally, on a stage and who were trying to become a working company too quickly.

The young dancers who had been selected from hundreds of applicants for the corps were mainly senior students from the School of American Ballet. One of their most respected teachers, Alexandra Danilova, often sat in the middle of the first row, first balcony, to watch what her charges could and could not do in a professional setting. Sometimes she looked genuinely proud . . . and she had good reason for her pride. Many of the young dancers, most still in their mid-teens, and many not finished with their training, looked just fine—as individuals. But she often shook her head; her students did not look right as a group. One of the major tasks any large-scale ballet company faces is to develop a corps. This takes time, more time than developing a repertory, finding the right costumes and scene designers, getting a good lighting expert, or even engaging the right principals for certain roles. Makarova has shown that she could take an existing corps that, over the years, had been allowed to go slack (the ABT group Croce mentioned in her review) and transform it into an accurate, exciting group. But taking some youngsters who had never worked together except in student performances and turning them into professionals in a matter of weeks required a miracle that no one, including even one of the best women dancers and teachers of her time, could perform.

The company danced only a brief New York season and was dissolved. Makarova went back to the American Ballet Theater where she proceeded to stage the whole of the Petipa ballet, *La Bayadere* (previously she had staged only one act), and everyone breathed a sigh of relief.

Since then, she has danced with ABT and done guest appearances with several European companies. She dances most the roles she knows best: the classics—and in those parts she is extraordinary. She is also remarkable in the one outstanding ballet created for her in the United States: *Other Dances,* by Jerome Robbins. Robbins made the pas de deux especially for Makarova and Baryshnikov for a special benefit performance for the Lincoln Center Dance Library. Robbins has a unique ability to suit a specific choreography to a dancer's capacities and style. *Other Dances,* to a series of piano pieces by Chopin, is classical ballet with definite Russian folk overtones. It uses the great classical style that both Russians acquired during their training with the Kirov, plus a certain kind of joy and informality that they seem to have gained in the United States. The ballet was filmed for television in a PBS special called *Two Duets.* It is still rerun frequently on educational TV channels throughout the United States, and anyone who is interested in dancing should watch program guides for one of these repeat performances. The ballet is a delight and shows both Makarova and Baryshnikov at the top of their respective forms.

In her career, Makarova has also disproved another one of those old ballet axioms that are constantly repeated but often turn out not to be true. It *is* possible for a ballerina to come back to ballet after having had a baby. If anything, Makarova looked better the first year she returned after the birth of André than she did before she took her maternity leave. Pregnancy and childbirth had done nothing to hamper her beautiful body line and may have added warmth and a certain kind of humanity to her already flawless classical performances.

She is now in her forties and still dancing at the top of her form. Rudolf Nureyev, who left the Kirov at the same time she did, is also still dancing; but by now he is clearly hampered by injuries and age. She would be the first to agree that there are certain advantages to being a woman if one wishes to make ballet a career. Women dancers, generally, last longer. Since they don't have to catch their partners in midair, their backs and knees are not as easily injured. There is also a kind of tapering off in speed and agility that seems to be possible for women dancers, but not for men. Women can change their roles. They can do fewer pirouettes, remain a little closer to the stage in their jumps and, as long as they keep their beautiful line and stay with the music, they will continue to function well as dancers. Actually, Makarova has not yet been forced to modify many of her roles, but she will be able to do so in the future and still look like the great dancer she is.

What's more, she has already proved that, given a reasonably good company (even one that has allowed its corps to relax its standards), she is able to stage ballets, especially the Petipa classics, as well as anyone alive today. Many of these ballets, as performed here and in Europe, could use the kind of restructuring and polishing that Makarova does so well. In fact, the companies who need her touch most are the Kirov and the Bolshoi, which have allowed their classic repertories to become even more dusty and musty than major American or European ballet companies. That she would be allowed to work in her former country, however, is, of course, highly unlikely.

Her influence on ballet here and in Europe has already been great. Because she has been able to dance the classic roles with the kind of traditional style and intensity that dancers not trained in Russia rarely have been able to achieve, she has managed to make ballets, that for many of us had become dull and even boring, suddenly interesting again. Since ballet is an art of tradition, an art that requires that technique, style and interpretation be handed down from one generation of great dancers to the next, Makarova's presence in the West means that she can be a link in the chain, bringing what once was best in Russian ballet to this country and Europe. All her students say she is a great, if often very difficult, teacher. Great teachers make new ballet stars. And some of those future stars will undoubtedly have received their final bit of polish, that extra ingredient that turns a good performance into a great one, in one of the classes or coaching sessions given by Natalia Makarova, who combines her Russian heritage with her personal and professional experience in the United States.

CHAPTER XXIII

Cynthia Gregory

There are great Russian dancers, but there are great American dancers too. Yet if you defect from San Francisco, nobody cares.

—CYNTHIA GREGORY in an interview for the *Saturday Review*, by dance critic, Walter Terry.

I F CYNTHIA GREGORY had been born in Leningrad, she probably would have danced all the same roles as Natalia Makarova there. The two women don't look alike. Gregory is tall for a dancer and relatively big-boned. Makarova is small with a tiny bone structure. Gregory looks regal; Makarova looks fragile. But even at the American Ballet Theater, where the two women are the reigning ballerinas, each apparently with her own group of fans, they are often assigned the same parts. They do a very different (from each other) *Swan Lake.* In fact, if it were not for the story, the music, the costumes, and the rest of the cast, one might think one was watching two different ballets. However differently the two dancers interpret the role of the princess-turned-into-a-swan, both interpretations are valid, and both dance exceedingly well . . . again, with a difference.

There simply is no way that Gregory is ever going to look fragile. She hasn't a fragile bone in her body. Even in *Giselle,* in which the heroine is supposed to die from a combination of a weakening illness and a broken heart, one often has the feeling that Gregory's Giselle drops dead out of sheer anger and frustration. But, again, the interpretation works. She also dances a smashing Aurora in *Sleeping Beauty*, remaining on point effortlessly while four different princes try to win her hand in marriage. (Some ballerinas find it hard to stay on point through *two* princes.)

There are some ballets, however, in which she really has no equal. The first is *Don Quixote* (not the Balanchine version made for Farrell, but a completely different ballet choreographed by Petipa and restaged for ABT by Baryshnikov). The ballet has the subtitle, *Kitri's Wedding*, which is a much more accurate description of the story. The choreography is principally about a young barber called Basil who is in love with a village girl called Kitri. Kitri's father wishes his daughter to marry a rich old man, Gamache. Kitri prefers Basil, and the two take off for a gypsy camp in the woods. They are caught and brought back home, where Gamache is waiting to marry Kitri. Basil fakes a very melodramatic suicide, and Don Quixote (who has been seen off and on only around the edge of the action, in spite of the fact that the ballet bears his name) convinces the father that Kitri should be allowed to marry Basil, who is, after all, dead and will, therefore, make her an instant widow. The marriage is performed with a very undead Basil, who rises to claim his wife. At the end, everybody forgives everybody, and the last act, as so many ballets' last acts do, features a wedding scene, complete with divertissements and a stunning pas de deux by the two lovers.

This ballet makes even less sense than many other Petipa stories, and the score by Ludwig Minkus sounds straight out of music by Muzak. But that final pas de deux can be worth the price of the ticket, and when Gregory dances it, it always is.

In the past several seasons she has also managed to outshine all competitors in yet another and completely different role, The Temptress in *The Prodigal Son*. This ballet is one of the few Balanchine choreographies that does indeed have a story—and the story is straight out of the Bible. The Prodigal leaves his loving father's home (Balanchine also gives him two gentle and dutiful sisters) to "waste his substance" in a foreign land, full of sin and sinners. Chief among the sinners is a woman, the Temptress, who literally winds the willful but innocent young man around her waist, seduces him and destroys him by turning him over to her friends to rob and torture. The son returns home, broken and repentant, and the father lovingly takes him back.

Gregory, as The Temptress, is like a gigantic man-eating orchid, cold, venomous and infernally attractive. Anyone in the audience can see why the son, danced in the ABT version, as it was in the New York City Ballet, by Baryshnikov, would succumb to her. And there is also no doubt that in spite of her haughty beauty, she is evil incarnate. The combination of the tall, regal Gregory and the rather small, agile Baryshnikov is electric.

In fact, it is unfortunate that there are not more roles in ballet that allow a relatively small man to dance with a relatively tall woman. One of Gregory's problems at ABT has been that she can make men her own size, or even taller, seem to disappear. There are balletomanes who dream of seeing Gregory dance with someone not only her own size, but also with her kind of dazzle and glamour. Peter Martins has often been mentioned. Unfortunately, ballet has its politics and alliances. And City Ballet dancers just don't move across the Lincoln Center Plaza to dance with ABT ballerinas. What's more, the princes with names like Albrecht *(Giselle)* or Siegfried *(Swan Lake)* or Florimund *(Sleeping Beauty)* don't interest Martins at all. They never have, which is one of the reasons he left Denmark for Balanchine.

In spite of the fact that she has often indicated her disagreement with ABT policies that, she says, seem to favor almost any Russian over any American, Gregory is now one of the two top ballerinas in that company. The only other female dancer who receives star treatment, in a company that does indeed still believe in stars, is Makarova. Gelsey Kirkland, another American dancer with very special promise, has danced very little in the past few years and is not expected to dance with ABT at all during the 1982 season.

Gregory came to ABT from the San Francisco Ballet in whose school she was trained. She made it from corps to principal in two years, which set a record. For a ballerina, she is not only technically excellent, she is also almost incredibly assertive. Ballerinas are supposed to do what they are told. They are called "girls" until they stop dancing, which may not be until they are about fifty years old. There is nothing particularly sexist about this—male dancers are called "boys" throughout their professional lives. But Gregory never behaved like a girl—she acted like a *woman* almost from the start. When she considered one ballet particularly vulgar, she came out on stage smoking a cigarette, stubbed it out with her toe shoe and was told by the then artistic director, Lucia Chase, that she would never be allowed to do that particular choreography again. She indicated that that was exactly what she had in mind when she made her contemptuous gesture.

In December of 1975, after several years as a top dancer in the company, she suddenly decided that she had had enough: too many restrictions, too much discipline, too many pressures. She went home to California, stopped going to class, gained weight and acted as if she had no intention of ever going back. She also, at that time, divorced her first husband and married again.

Apparently the second marriage allowed her to find enough inner strength and conviction to return to dancing. She lost the weight she needed to lose, got back into shape and, by December of 1976, was back with ABT. She has been there ever since. Because she is only in her middle thirties, she can be expected to outlast any female Russian presently on the scene.

She has said, repeatedly and loudly, that in her opinion, there is no conflict between a happy marriage and a career in ballet. "The conflict in *Turning Point*, which indicates that a dancer either has to become a frumpy housewife or a lonely, aging dancer, is nonsense," she said in one interview. She has also indicated that one day, not too far away, she would like to have a child—and then go on dancing.

For the 1982 spring season, ABT is tentatively planning to present the ballet *Carmen* by French choreographer Roland Petit. It's a Kitri type of role in which she could really shine.

Gregory also seems to mean what she says about the growing importance of American ballet for Americans. She has danced, probably for considerably less money than she could earn by guest appearances in Europe and South America, with any number of small regional American companies. She helps them raise funds and encourages young dancers to stay in their profession even when the odds of stardom are rather small. She may not exactly say: "Look, I'm out of the American West . . . not the European ballet . . . and I made it . . . so you can too," but her very presence as a top female dancer in a star-conscious company like ABT seems to make that point.

At ABT, more than at any other ballet company, individual

dancers have their special fans in the audience. And at ABT, those fans may be wearing mink coats and designer clothes, but they sometimes have a tendency to behave like groupies. Gregory fans have two special qualities: they indicate their approval by shouting loudly "Brava" (which is female for "Bravo"); and from the four balconies at the Metropolitan Opera House, where ABT dances when the company is at Lincoln Center, they shower shredded programs over the audience in the orchestra seats and onto the stage. (After the performance is over, of course.) It's a sort of indoor ticker tape parade. It may make extra work for the cleanup crew, but Gregory almost always deserves it.

CHAPTER XXIV

Jacques d'Amboise

Dancing transformed his life, and that is why Jacques d'Amboise, a big American boy, with an aristocratic French name and a ballet technique that is elegantly and peculiarly Russian, has become in his mid-forties a missionary of the dance, a symbol of virile grace for the New York City Ballet. . . . He now dreams of sweeping into rhythmic self-expression all the youth of America—for dancing, he believes, is every child's cultural birthright.

—BARBARA GELB in an article in
The New York Times magazine section.

For the first time in his life, Bruce feels unselfconscious, just like a normal little boy. He has been partially deaf, and he was very shy around other children, even though he can lip read and he talks almost normally. But, thanks to Jacques, he now knows he can also dance. *He can even perform at this huge dance recital. . . . It has turned his life around. . . .*

—The mother of one boy in the group of deaf children
performing at a benefit for Jacques d'Amboise's
National Dance Institute
at the Felt Forum,
Madison Square Garden, New York City
in 1981.

U NTIL RECENTLY, Jacques d'Amboise was one of Balanchine's great male dancers. He had a massive body, which few men in ballet possess, topped by the face of an elf with black, curly hair. His skill as a partner was legendary. He could jump higher and do more air turns than any other man in the company and also managed to look just fine in a number of Hollywood movies. That large, boyish man, jumping fences with inches of space to spare, in the film *Seven Brides For Seven Brothers* is the Jacques d'Amboise of many years ago, earning the extra money he needed for his growing family. The movie is still shown these days, occasionally on television. So are some of the other movies in which d'Amboise danced: *Carousel* with its Agnes de Mille choreography, and *The Best Things in Life Are Free.*

But most of d'Amboise's life has been spent with the New York City Ballet, which he joined in 1949, and which, several years ago, gave him an affectionate thirty-year anniversary celebration. D'Amboise danced *Meditation,* made for him and Suzanne Farrell, who, many years ago, as Sue Flicker, had clipped his pictures out of magazines. Many of his long-time fans gave him an ovation. Some may have wiped a few nostalgic tears from their eyes.

He still dances a few roles with the company: the leader of a Scottish clan and, later in the ballet, a fun-loving sailor in Balanchine's salute to Great Britain, *Union Jack.* The day the Iranian hostages were returned to the United States, Balanchine put on a special performance of *Stars and Stripes.* Uncle Sam was, fittingly enough, Jacques d'Amboise.

His most important role in the 1981–82 season was the leading man in *Who Cares?* to the show-stopping Gershwin tunes that he loves. In that ballet he gets to dance with all three of the lead ballerinas and has a fast and furious solo variation of his own in which he shows that he can still do those fast air turns and splits. It brings down the house . . . every time. And dancing behind him in the corps is his son Christopher d'Amboise who joined the company several years ago and who is beginning to get some important solos of his own.

There was a performance of *Union Jack* in which d'Amboise

was hurt slightly doing his solo role as a sailor. He disappeared into the wings and Chris came out to finish the solo. At the end of the performance, Chris ran out and Jacques limped out. Again, they brought down the house.

But what he does mostly these days is to bring the joy of dancing to more than a thousand children who attend public and parochial schools in New York City and a few surrounding communities. Many of the youngsters are black and Puerto Rican. Some are handicapped. A few years ago, d'Amboise talked to a speech therapist who told him that even deaf children were usually not entirely without hearing. They might be able to sense a rhythm, particularly if the rhythmical notes were low on the scale, like the beat of a kettle drum. Also, they seemed to feel vibrations given by sounds more sensitively than children who were not hearing-impaired. So d'Amboise decided to add to his program a special class for deaf youngsters. Apparently his system works. The children, in their first performance, at a benefit for the National Dance Institute in Madison Square Garden, looked like dancing children, not dancing deaf children. His program, unlike that of the School of American Ballet, is not designed to produce professional dancers, although out of the hordes of little boys and girls who sign up for his classes, some professionals may eventually emerge. He always starts enlisting *boys* first, because, he says, if he includes girls from the beginning, only girls would sign up. So, after he has enlisted enough young males, he expands the program to girls as well. First, he establishes that dancing is something that is as masculine as football, basketball or ice hockey and can be a great deal more fun.

Watching d'Amboise with children is an experience that few forget. The children all call him Jacques. For many, he seems to be the big brother they dreamed of but never had. He is warm and loving, but also exacting. "You are *dancers*," he tells a rambunctious group of nine-year-olds who are wrestling on the floor or pushing each other around playfully, giggling or throwing spit balls, when they should be paying attention to whatever dance routine he is showing them. "*Dancers* have good manners," he says. "*Dancers* pay attention. *Dancers* don't kid around when they should be dancing." His voice sounds fierce, and then he grins. The boys grin back and settle down to their practice session.

244

D'Amboise grew up on the New York streets, in the kind of neighborhood that could be the backdrop for Robbins's *West Side Story*. His father was an often unemployed telegrapher by the name of Andrew Patrick Ahearn. His mother was a dreamy, romantic, yet somehow practical French Canadian called Georgette d'Amboise. Somehow, d'Amboise sounded better as a dancer's name than Ahearn. So Jacques, when he became a professional dancer, adopted it for himself and for his own family.

She had told her son about dances that were performed at royal courts, of fairy tales with princes and princesses and swans that turned into beautiful maidens. That was her fanciful side. Then she took young Jacques, at age eight, to the School of American Ballet for a scholarship. That was her practical side. And Jacques became hooked on dance almost immediately. By the time he was nine, he was excused early from parochial school to go to ballet class. And, just in case anyone in school considered him a sissy, he could always show them with his fists, if necessary, that ballet did not just make you graceful, it also made you strong and agile.

Today, he may have the courtly manners of a dancer of the old school, but those manners are mixed with a definite New York accent and infectious good humor that sometimes breaks through in unexpected ways. One feels that he has been influenced by Balanchine in many aspects of his life, aristocratic bearing included. But the New York streets are as much a part of his personality as the courtly manners of the ballet world. He has often remarked: "In my part of town, half the boys became gangsters and the other half cops." Because the children he teaches come mainly from those streets, they sense, in a way that never seems to need an explanation, that he is really one of them, just a little older, and that they can trust him. Often it is evident that the feelings he evokes in his young students are more than trust: it's pure love, going in both directions.

He teaches by demonstration. He jumps, he twirls, he sings, he stomps his feet. He lifts his arms, with their beautiful hands that even Balanchine has praised, and shows the boys and girls how to position their fingers. He does this in exactly the same way when he teaches a would-be ballerina in the NYCB corps how she can improve her "port de bras" (the ballet way of describing how arms and hands should be held). "My arms have always been my best dancing feature," he tells an interviewer.

"My feet were bad. I tried, but there was not much I could do
about them, except wear shoes that made them look more graceful, and that often were too tight. Maybe that's why I have arthritis today."

He still takes class and dances when he can. Every day he
starts by jogging. "If I didn't start moving early in the morning,
my arthritis could get the better of me and I might never be able
to move again," he told interviewer Dick Cavett on a show during which he and his son, Chris, improvised a dance for three
men: one with a broken leg. Cavett had his foot in a cast after a
bad fall. The choreography was funny, and it certainly got Cavett
out of his chair. "Always move; it's good for you," d'Amboise
told him.

Every year the National Dance Institute's program at Madison Square Garden includes something new. There are celebrities, many of them long-time friends: Judy Collins one year, Mary
Tyler Moore another. There are dancers from NYCB: Patricia
McBride, Karin von Aroldingen, and others. Baryshnikov, for instance. Everybody performs. But, two years ago, d'Amboise apparently remembered those boys in his neighborhood who joined
the police. Couldn't the benefits of dance be spread to New
York's Finest as well as all those children?

So he put up notices in several police stations, recruiting
dancers for the show. About two dozen showed up at the first
rehearsal and learned their dance. Karin von Aroldingen was the
leading lady. George Balanchine composed the music for the
choreography made by d'Amboise. And, two years later, one of
those policemen was taking class at a professional school. He has
not made it into the School of American Ballet yet, but he is
trying, he said.

Today, d'Amboise and his wife, Carolyn, a former dancer
who teaches and does ballet photography under the professional
name of Carolyn George, live with three of their four children in
a large brownstone house on New York's West Side, near Lincoln
Center. His oldest son is in the Air Force. Chris is with NYCB
and the twin daughters are still in school. Besides the d'Amboise
youngsters, their friends and several youngsters from one of the
New York City classes that always seem to be around Jacques,
there are usually many young students from the School of American Ballet all over the house. Some live there, from the time
they come to New York City until they decide to move, which

246

may be a few weeks or a few months, depending on what housing arrangements they can make. "The place can be a madhouse," one of the young dancers said. "But it's the warmest, most loving madhouse I've ever been in."

For d'Amboise, life apparently started at eight, and has continued full blast into his forties, around the profession he truly loves: dance. For him, dance has meant everything that it has to most of the other dancers in this book: beauty, joy, pain, hardships, discipline, some fame and a limited kind of financial security. But to him, dance also has meant something more: a gift, a blessing that he wishes to return to others. Dance, he feels, gave him the life he wanted. What dance gave him, he is now trying to give to over a thousand New York children to whom little else may be given by a society that keeps telling us it loves children as a group, but at the same time, seems unwilling to put itself out for an individual boy or girl. D'Amboise cares for children: individually as well as in groups. He shows it when he teaches his classes in inner city schools; when he scours a sold-out New York State Theater to find a few empty seats for some of those children, who may not ever have seen a live ballet; and when he takes young dancers into his house so that they can get a chance to study at the same ballet school that trained him. D'Amboise has class, imagination and a sense of what is really important in life. Those qualities helped to make him a good dancer. They also make him a very good man. And, just as an added attraction, he may be developing, among all those children he shows what dance is all about, a dance audience for the future.

Even when he isn't flying,
Baryshnikov looks like no one else.
Here he is
in Balanchine's Apollo.

It's a bird; it's a plane;
it's Baryshnikov . . .
here dancing the role of
the Prodigal Son.

Suzanne Farrell and Peter Martins
are one of the magic
partnerships in ballet.
Here they are together
in the last act of **The Nutcracker.**

All's well that ends well . . .
Peter Martins in
the wedding pas de deux
in **Coppelia.**

*Suzanne Farrell, looking haunted,
mysterious and incredibly
beautiful in the last section
of* Vienna Waltzes.

Patricia McBride
is the right size and shape
to be cast as a ballerina doll.
Here she is in that role in
Balanchine's **The Steadfast Tin Soldier.**
The leader of the regiment is
Baryshnikov.
The rest of the soldiers are
made of cardboard.

Natalia Makarova in La Sylphide,
looking appropriately sylphlike.

*Patricia McBride in Balanchine's
salute to Gershwin:* Who Cares?

*If Cynthia Gregory had not decided
to become a dancer,
she probably could have won
an Olympic broad jump competition.
Here she is in a Danish classic
ballet,* Napoli.

*Jacques d'Amboise as Don Quixote,
with Suzanne Farrell.
When she was a child she used to dance
with a chair and pretend
the furniture was d'Amboise.*

Conclusion

CHAPTER XXV

Where Do We Go from Here?

Dancers work and live from the inside. They are almost always in pain, physically and mentally. The responsibility of keeping in shape is never ending and crushing. They can never let down. The intensity of behavior, which laymen find trying, is, for the dancer, essential. They drive themselves constantly, producing a glow that lights not only themselves, but audience after audience. They personify life itself. . . .

May I propose a toast. "To dancers. For whatever personal hell you may go through. For whatever professional calamity may be heaped upon you. For whatever comfort this may bring, be assured you are not alone. You are *the profession. Without you there is no dance."*

—MURRAY LOUIS, dancer, choreographer and teacher
in his book *Inside Dance.*

In AN ECONOMIC FORECAST for the decade of the eighties, *The New York Times* listed the jobs that would require more professionals in the future. We would need fewer teachers and social workers, for instance, the *Times* suggested. We would need *more* dancers.

One can only hope that that economic prophecy was more correct than such prophecies usually are, because all indications point to the fact that there will be even *fewer* jobs for professional dancers in the coming years. And some of those dancers may need a somewhat different education than they are now getting. They will be dancing less on ballet stages and at cultural centers and more in television studios, and, probably, in the movies. We may need fewer classical dancers perhaps and more dancers who can perform in a number of different styles. Right now, dancers are doing everything from television commercials (for blue jeans, soap and linoleum floors) to special guest performances at the White House. But where the Carters picked some of the top performers in classical ballet to entertain their state visitors, the Reagans are using show dancers, dancers who have appeared in musical comedy on Broadway and the movies.

The ballet and modern dance explosion may be extinguished by the budget crunch. Regional dance companies that have provided jobs for the thousands of young people graduating from American ballet schools may have to fold up or curtail their schedules to the point where their dancers will no longer be eligible for unemployment benefits. And a dancer who is not yet a star, doing guest performances all over the world, and who is not eligible for unemployment compensation, will probably have to change professions.

Funds for the National Endowment for the Arts are drying up. Even if some of us can persuade the Congress to stop being extra generous to Pentagon-sponsored military bands (which, as we have noted, got more federal money in 1982 than all the arts, including dance, put together) and to use some of those funds for dance companies, there still will be a shortage of money. State Councils for the Arts are even more hard-pressed than the National Endowment, and the tax laws have been rewritten in such a way that the very rich and the corporations no longer need the tax deductions that are allowed them for financial support to the arts. They will be paying lower taxes in any case.

Dance companies, if they wish to stay alive, will have to do a lot more fund-raising on their own. All those *Nutcrackers* will no longer be enough. Their fund-raising efforts will have to become a lot more sophisticated. After all, they are competing for the public's shrinking dollars with organizations that range from the United Way and Red Cross campaigns to the fund drives put on by local Little Leagues; from the American Civil Liberties Union to the Moral Majority; from the United Nations' UNICEF to the neighborhood garden clubs. And dance companies have never been very good at fund-raising. One often gets the impression that they consider talk of money a little vulgar. In the future, a good money-raiser will be almost as necessary to a thriving company as a superb artistic director.

Dance groups are going to have to attract special volunteers who have had training in public relations, or even hire professionals who know this field. Even the best-known companies sometimes write the kind of fund-raising letters that belong in the *New Yorker* magazine section of "Letters we never finished reading."

Let's take one received very recently from the American Ballet Theater. This is how ABT's appeal, supposedly written by Artistic Director Mikhail Baryshnikov, and signed by him on a photo offset stencil, began: "The hour is late. I have just partnered Cynthia Harvey* in *Swan Lake* here in Detroit and I am nearly too exhausted to write. But I have been meaning to draft this letter for weeks, and it is far too important to delay any longer. So as Tschaikovsky's magnificent score echoes in my mind, I have turned my thoughts to home and to you . . ."

The letter ends by urging "the friend" (to whom it is addressed) to "Embrace us. . . ."

Somewhere in the middle of this letter, there is a sentence one would tend to overlook, unless one were writing a ballet book and, therefore, reading any communications from dance companies with extra care. "Anyone who contributes money to the company may attend some open rehearsals and may be able to see Baryshnikov either dancing or teaching in an informal setting." Now that's a good reason for any balletomane to make a contribution.

The chances of seeing the artistic director in action, rather

---

* Cynthia Harvey is an ABT dancer whom Baryshnikov frequently partners.

than just a few raw recruits from the corps are, of course, slim. But the chances of winning a state lottery are rather slim too, and still people buy lottery tickets.

But anyone who knows anything at all about dance in general, and Baryshnikov in particular, also knows that the whole idea of a major ballet star, after an exhausting performance (in a role he has said he dislikes), going up to a lonely hotel room in Detroit to write a fund drive letter is so unlikely as to be almost endearing. Anybody who has ever met Baryshnikov, or for that matter, has seen him dance, knows that the man has too much dignity to go around letting himself be embraced by strangers, even with the help of a photo offset machine.

During the same week that ABT sent out its plea for money, NYCB mailed out one of its own. The text of the communication made a great deal more sense. It was straightforward: told why the company needed money and how this year's dollars would be used. There was only one thing wrong with the appeal. It was dated November 17, received December 18, and its first sentence said: "Tonight the New York City Ballet opens its 75th season." By the time those letters were mailed, that season was half over. One wonders what would happen to a dancer who got to class, just once, as late as those letters got into our mailboxes.

The ABT and the NYCB letters are no exceptions. Many other dance companies don't do as well. But the time has come for the arts to take public relations as seriously as the Salvation Army or the International Business Machine Corporation already do.

"Probably no form of hucksterism is as embarrassing as cultural hucksterism," says Arlene Croce in *Afterimages*. "Everyone knows that ballet is too expensive to support itself on box office alone. The devious sales pitches serve no purpose; they fool no one. The thing that sold ballet to the American public is ballet itself." How right she is!

Most of us realize, somewhere deep inside ourselves, that life without art would diminish us as individuals and as citizens. That's one of the reasons Jacques d'Amboise teaches almost a thousand boys and girls every year in inner city schools, and why Baryshnikov dances at benefits to help small, regional dance companies that don't have the kind of star who attracts wealthy patrons willing to spend $500 on a ticket with a chance to meet a superdancer. It is also one of the reasons why, no matter how

264

deeply funds for the arts are cut by government, they will, most probably, not be eliminated entirely. Even legislators who are not generally seen in concert halls, at poetry readings or at a ballet performance know that we need a few roses along with our daily bread.

Whether the money comes from the government, from private foundations or from people who just love dance and are willing to support it to the best of their abilities, there is one place from which it can no longer come and that is from the dancers. Dancers have been supporting their art to an extent that few other professionals have ever done. They have worked incredible hours for not nearly enough money or security, and with almost none of the benefits all types of workers now expect as a matter of course in the United States. The corps dancers who were locked out of their practice and rehearsal rooms by the American Ballet Theater showed that they had, finally, had enough. They did not return to the company until they were paid enough to sustain themselves in New York City, not luxuriously, perhaps not even adequately, but at least without having to ask their families or their friends to help out with basic necessities.

One practice that has kept dancers in their places is calling them "boys" and "girls" long after they have stopped being teenagers. Lourdes Lopez and Maria Calegari are not girls. They are women. Joe Duell and Peter Frame are not boys, they are men. Referring to them as perpetual adolescents makes it possible to underpay them. After all, kids only need pocket money, don't they? And the practice also denies them the respect that is due them. Nobody calls a young intern at a hospital or an assistant cashier at a bank, or a football coach, a boy. No one (at least no one with any sense of fairness) calls a young attorney, an advertising account executive or a junior high school teacher a girl. Dancer Gelsey Kirkland, although she was a principal of ABT at the time of the lockout, picketed with the corps members and made that point. She and everyone on the picket line had a right to be just as angry as they were.

Even if we find ways of raising more money for dance, and if we begin to respect the professional standards of the dancers, there will probably still not be enough work in the traditional dance fields for the many gifted and dedicated young men and women who graduate from our best dance schools every year. But dance is becoming an integral part of television. Not only the public broadcast stations and the culture cable stations are now showing us dancers, they appear on network prime time, in specials, in variety shows and in advertisements. Even a soap opera recently had a dancer as one of the principal characters; she danced as a regular part of the plot, as well as suffering and drinking endless cups of coffee like all the other characters on the show.

Boards of directors of prestigious dance companies sometimes try to discourage appearances by dancers on commercial programs as undignified and demeaning. But then few board members ever have to worry about paying the rent or buying enough nourishing, high-protein food to sustain their health. If a dancer can make extra money in a commercial venture, he or she should not just be allowed, but encouraged to do so, just as long as the venture does not present a real conflict of interest to the company or is in especially bad taste.

Recently the Joffrey Company, which was in especially dire financial straits, collaborated with Rudolf Nureyev on his Broadway program (and eventual PBS-TV show), *A Tribute to Diaghilev.* There were all kinds of snide remarks made by people who should have known better, about how the Joffrey was engaged in a "rent-a-company" policy. The venture probably kept the company going for that year—and, what's more, the project was artistically, as well as financially, successful. One wanted to ask the critics if they would be willing to finance that very fine American dance company for a year if the management decided to turn down the Nureyev offer as too commercial.

One can also hope that there will be many more movies like *The Turning Point,* which show the best of ballet, along with a story that is interesting enough to make the film a hit.

Certainly many Broadway shows, like *A Chorus Line* and *42nd Street,* will become motion pictures within the foreseeable future. Then a much larger public than the regular New York theater audience will be exposed to the best of Broadway and jazz dancing and might be willing to support it. And the success these shows have had in the theater seems to insure that more shows with dancing at their core will be staged in the years to come.

No one really knows where classical ballet will be going in the coming years. We do know, however, that importing Russian or any other type of international stars, paying them huge salaries and neglecting native talent is a practice on its way out. Baryshnikov has told the ABT Board of Directors that he does not intend to hire guest stars: "you are either part of the company or you are not." And he has also indicated that he intends to create his own principal dancers by allowing talented young men and women from the corps to advance as quickly as possible, by giving them solo roles almost as soon as they are taken on by the company. Balanchine has never believed in inviting guests to dance with NYCB . . . and whoever follows him will almost certainly feel the same way.

What's more, the pool of foreign, or more specifically, Russian superstars is running dry. Anyone who saw the Bolshoi Ballet dance in the United States during that company's most recent tour realized that the United States is training better dancers now. There were very few ballerinas in the Russian company who could compare to the best principals in such companies as NYCB, ABT, the Pennsylvania Ballet and the San Francisco Ballet, to name just a few. Among the men there was no one who danced better than many of the principal dancers of the Dance Theater of Harlem or the Alvin Ailey Company. In fact, artistic directors of formerly all-white companies have taken serious looks at these two groups in particular. And the success that Mel Tomlinson, a dancer from the Harlem ballet company, had in 1982 with NYCB will probably remind any number of ballet company managers that the largest and best pool of male dancers in the world is home-grown and home-trained, somewhere near 125th Street and Lexington Avenue in New York City.

There is an usher at the New York State Theater, Charlotte Thyssen, a slender blonde woman in her fifties, who was once, in her native Germany, a well-known dancer. She is an usher now because that's the only way she can watch as many dance performances as she wishes. Occasionally, she still gets a small character part with a dance company that needs to fill out its corps for crowd scenes. She has seen excellent dancers come and go over the years, and every year, as she sees one American dance company after another, she says: "You know, they get better all the time." They do . . . and still dancers, in class and rehearsal rooms throughout this country, will go on trying for the perfect arabesque, the perfect jump, the perfect pirouette, which will always be somehow just out of reach. The search for unattainable perfection is the one essential ingredient in dancing that no other profession consistently requires or even expects. That's what makes dancers, as individuals and as a group, different from the rest of us. It is also the reason they have a right to expect, from us, what they so richly deserve: enough money to live on, a chance to work at their profession and the same status as other highly trained and gifted professional artists. They also deserve the kind of respect and admiration that those who do their very best, but still, always try to do a little better, should get from those whose lives are enriched by their contribution to the world.

Bibliography

BALANCHINE, GEORGE and MASON, FRANCIS: *Complete Stories of the Great Ballets*, Doubleday, Garden City, N.Y., 1978

BARYSHNIKOV, MIKHAIL: *Baryshnikov at Work*, Alfred A. Knopf, New York, 1978.

BLAND, ALEXANDER: *A History of Ballet and Dance*, Praeger Publishers, Inc., New York, 1976.

BUCKLE, RICHARD: *Diaghilev*, Atheneum, New York, 1979.

CHUJOY, ANATOLE AND MANCHESTER, P. W.: *The Dance Encyclopedia*, Simon and Schuster, New York, 1967.

CRISP, CLEMENT AND THORP, EDWARD: *Ballet*, Octopus Book Limited, London, 1977.

CROCCE, ARLENE: *Afterimages*, Vintage Books, New York, 1977.

DE MILLE, AGNES: *America Dances*, Macmillan, New York, 1980.

————*Promenade Home*, Da Capo, New York, 1980.

————*To a Young Dancer, Little Brown & Co. 1960.*

DENBY, EDWIN: *Dancers, Buildings and People in the Streets*, Popular Library, New York, 1965.

FISHER, JOHN: *The Legends: Twelve All-Time Great Entertainers*, Stein and Day, New York, 1976.

FRANCISCO, CHARLES: *The Radio City Music Hall*, E. P. Dutton, New York, 1979.

GRAHAM, MARTHA: *The Notebooks of Martha Graham*, Harcourt, Brace Jovanovich, New York, 1973.

GRUEN, JOHN: *The World's Great Ballets*, N. Abrams Inc., New York, 1981.

HODGSON, MOIRA: *Quintet: Five American Dance Companies*, William Morrow and Company, New York, 1976.

269

KERSLEY, LEO AND SINCLAIR, JANET: *A Dictionary of Ballet Terms*, DaCapo, New York, 1979.

KIRSTEIN, LINCOLN: *Lincoln Kirstein's Thirty Years, The New York City Ballet*, Alfred A. Knopf, New York, 1978.

LAZZARINI, JOHN AND ROBERTA: *Pavlova: Repertoire of a Legend*, Schirmer Books, New York, 1980.

LOUIS, MURRAY: *Inside Dance*, St. Martin's, New York, 1980.

MAGRIEL, PAUL (edited by): *Chronicles of American Dance*, DaCapo, New York, 1978 (paperback).

MAY, ROBIN: *Discovering Ballet*, Marshall Cavendish, London, 1979.

MAZO, JOSEPH H.: *Dance Is a Contact Sport*, DaCapo, New York, 1976.

SIEGEL, MARCIA B.: *The Shapes of Change: Images of American Dance*, Houghton Mifflin, Boston, 1979.

Index